"There are countless men and women [...] painful effects of growing up without a [...] stand that pain! But in *The Father You've [...] wanted, Ed randy* McGlasson helps readers understand the healing and hope found in God, our heavenly Father."

—Jim Daly, president, Focus on the Family

"The strongest form of motivation is encouragement. Everyone needs to be encouraged constantly. *The Father You've Always Wanted* will motivate you to bless, encourage, and rally the people in your life. It is a healing book, full of remedies—a must read."

—Bill McCartney, founder and chairman emeritus, Promise Keepers

"I wish I could pass this book out to every dad I know. Ed is passionate about helping men become all they were meant to be. This book is a compelling read with very practical insight. Ed is one of my most favorite authorities on fathering and men issues."

—Jim Burns, PhD, president, HomeWord; author, *Creating an Intimate Marriage* and *Confident Parenting*

"Thanks, Ed, for writing this book. 'Performance-based approval' is the story of my life, and when you said, 'Performance-based approval is one of Satan's greatest weapons,' it hit home. Sadly I could look back and see that probably far too often I had unknowingly done the same things to my son as my dad did to me in how I reacted to various situations. The good news is this is a book of hope in that there is a Father who loves us—unconditionally. And it is never too late. I would encourage anyone who has ever felt they had to 'earn' the love of their parents by their performance to read this book!"

—Jim West, cofounder and managing partner, The Barnabas Group

"Absolutely life changing! Whether you feel you've failed as a father, or you've suffered from a harsh father who did not bless you, it's never too late. In the pages of this book, McGlasson maps a path to hope and healing. I pray that this book gets into the hands of every person who has never heard the words 'You are my beloved.'"

—**Ron Strand**, founder, The Upper Room Presents

"WOW! Unbelievably powerful is an understatement in how I would describe this treasure of a read. Within the first few chapters, through my tears, I said to myself, 'Every person on the face of the planet needs to hear this message!' *The Father You've Always Wanted* is a powerhouse and a must read. Its profound truth and penetrating impact has been deeply imbedded into the recesses of my heart, never to be forgotten. Outstanding, Ed, simply outstanding! May God continue to shine his face and blessings upon you, my friend."

—**Debbie Rasa**, owner/partner, Rasa Floors, LLC

The
FATHER
YOU'VE
ALWAYS
WANTED

The

FATHER
YOU'VE
ALWAYS
WANTED

HOW GOD *Heals* YOUR FATHER WOUNDS

ED TANDY MCGLASSON

BakerBooks

a division of Baker Publishing Group
Grand Rapids, Michigan

Published by Baker Books
a division of Baker Publishing Group
P.O. Box 6287, Grand Rapids, MI 49516-6287
www.bakerbooks.com

Printed in the United States of America

Library of Congress Cataloging-in-Publication Data is on file at the Library of Congress, Washington, DC.

ISBN 978-0-8010-1554-0

The internet addresses, email addresses, and phone numbers in this book are accurate at the time of publication. They are provided as a resource. Baker Publishing Group does not endorse them or vouch for their content or permanence.

Published in association with the literary agency of D.C. Jacobson & Associates, an Author Management Company, www.dcjacobson.com.

In keeping with biblical principles of creation stewardship, Baker Publishing Group advocates the responsible use of our natural resources. As a member of the Green Press Initiative, our company uses recycled paper when possible. The text paper of this book is composed in part of post-consumer waste.

16   17   18   19   7   6   5   4   3   2

green
press
INITIATIVE

I want to dedicate this book first to my beloved wife, Jill, who has loved me and has been my best friend for the last thirty years. Being loved by her is one of God's greatest gifts to me.

I also want to dedicate this book to my five beloved children who have taught me so much about being a dad. There is nothing more valuable to a dad than watching his kids become everything God wants them to be and to be invited by them to be a part of their unfolding story. Edward, Jessica, Mary Lee, Lukas, and Joshua—thank you for helping me become a father who makes a difference. It is a profound honor to be a part of the story your lives are writing for the glory of God.

And to every parent meeting the Father they have always wanted for the first time . . . this promise is for you:

> "Look around you and see, for all your children will
> come back to you. As surely as I live," says the LORD,
> "they will be like jewels or bridal ornaments for you
> to display."
>
> Isaiah 49:18 NLT

Contents

Acknowledgments

I want to thank my team at ETM Ministries for their prayer, support, wisdom, and love as we have together brought this message to tens of thousands of people these past years. Special thanks to Jimmy, Dac, Ron, Greg, Doug, Wayne, and their amazing wives. To Pam and Duffy, who encouraged me to communicate this message with excellence to a bigger audience.

To all my friends who have encouraged me to never stop sharing this message, and to Michael and Debbie Rasa, who have given away hundreds of copies of my first book to their friends that helped make this book possible.

I want to thank my assistant, Mary Pero, for her tireless editing and gift of writing. Your passion, insights, and gifts have added so much to this work.

To all of the churches, events, and conferences that have given me a place to share this message, thank you.

To my community at the Stadium Vineyard, who have walked with me these past twenty years as I was learning how to be fathered by God, thank you.

I want to also thank my agent Don Jacobson and editor David Jacobson for their support and brilliant work as we sat in a room and laid out this manuscript. Your friendship and encouragement have stretched me to become a better communicator.

I want to thank my new team at Baker Publishing Group for not only "getting this message" but also for your commitment to bring healing to those still stuck in the wounds of their father.

Finally, I want to thank You, Jesus, for introducing me to the Father I have always wanted. No wonder You lived with a smile on Your face. ☺

Introduction

We Need the Father's Blessing

Did you know that there is a castle in Southern California? The Castle, home and headquarters of Teen Challenge of Southern California, a ministry that provides faith-based solutions to teen addictions, isn't like the castles of Europe that you've seen in movies, full of knights and nobles. Instead, this castle is filled with spiritual orphans who have never known the love and blessing of a father.

I have enjoyed the privilege of speaking at many different venues these past years, but to tell you the truth, I have never witnessed the kind of hunger I saw one night in the Castle. It was clear from the first worship song that the room was filled with a gratitude that comes to those whose lives have been rescued from the gutter.

Tears were flowing soon after I began speaking that night. At the end of the message, I asked the crowd, "How many of you did not have a father who knew how to love and bless you?" There was a sea of hands all over the room, and before I finished the invitation to come forward, they rushed the stage. How many of these young lives had been set adrift because of not having a loving father? What they needed was a new Father, and Jesus came to give them that relationship.

The prophet Jeremiah described our generation best when he wrote, "Orphans we are, not a father in sight, and our mothers no better than widows" (Lam. 5:3 Message). Like many dads, my own early attempts at being a father failed miserably. I was raising PKs—pastor's kids—who were resenting the life and the ministry that I was living. Our family was broken because there was not a loving father present: me! What I needed was not another attempt at becoming a better dad. I needed a miracle in my heart. Without a blessing from my own father, I had little to give my kids. I needed an encounter with God the Father so that my heart could turn away from myself and toward my kids.

I have never met a dad or mom who didn't want their kids to have a better life. Yet they struggle to give the love and blessing they themselves are still waiting to receive from their own fathers. I spent many years trying to prove myself to replace the blessing that I never received from my father.

I met an eighty-three-year-old Jewish man who told me, "I was never blessed by my father as a young boy. All I ever wanted from my dad was for him to tell me one time that he loved me and that he was proud of me."

This man went on to tell me that he had lived his entire life trying to prove himself worthy of his father's love and never received it. *When fathers ache from the loss of their own father's love, it can set them on a path of doing the same things to the children they love.*

So how does God heal the wounds from your father?

Effort alone didn't work for me. My good intentions were short-lived. What I needed was an encounter with the only Father who could turn my wounds into a blessing.

It is time to stop beating up fathers and instead give them some tools and answers. It is my hope that this book is both miraculous and practical. It will be miraculous as you encounter the blessing of the Father for your own life—not in my power, or yours, but in God's—and practical in the many ways that you will be able to transfer that blessing to those you love. This book is for both men and women who are still missing the blessing that has eluded them.

The Bible says in Malachi that there will be a day when God will "turn the hearts of fathers to their children" (Mal. 4:6). I believe that we are in that day right now! Without the healing of men's hearts, we have little hope of turning the tide that is threatening to drown our families.

Jesus made a promise to His disciples before He went to the cross. He said, "I will not leave you as orphans; I will come to you" (John 14:18). The word He used for "orphan" is also translated "father-less." I am sure that many in that crowd did not understand why Jesus had just called everyone in that room "fatherless," especially since most of them lived within their father's community. Jesus was promising His followers the ultimate Father. The Father sent Jesus to unlock the door of our orphanage, and adopt us into His own perfectly loving family.

The key for the lock on that door is the blessing of the Father. While I was writing this book, Jesus dropped a Scripture into my heart: "The hour is coming when I will no longer speak to you in figures of speech but will tell you plainly about the Father" (John 16:25). I believe that we are in that hour! This book is the culmination of a ten-year conversation that Jesus has spoken into my heart, and I can't wait to share it with you.

One writer said it best: "If the written word of the Bible could be changed into a spoken word and become a single voice, this

voice, more powerful than the roaring of the sea would cry out:
'The Father loves you'"!¹

It is time to leave the orphanage and come home to the Father's
house. Jesus came to give us access to the Father that we have always
wanted. The same Father who loved Him before the foundation of
the world, the same Father who made a way for you and me to be
loved the same way He loved His only begotten Son.

> Jesus said these things. Then, raising his eyes in prayer, he said:
>
> > Father, it's time.
> > Display the bright splendor of your Son
> > So the Son in turn may show your bright splendor. . . .
> > And this is the real and eternal life:
> > *That they know you,*
> > The one and only true God [Father],
> > And Jesus Christ, whom you sent. (John 17:1, 3 Message,
> > emphasis mine)

A number of months ago I received an email message:

> A friend gave me your little book *The Difference a Father Makes*,
> and I am unable to get through it. I read 2–3 sentences and I am
> either stunned or can't see through my tears.
>
> I am a 41-yr-old vibrant Christian woman with many gifts, a
> master's degree, and wonderful friends. Men are interested in me
> though I can't seem to find Mr. Right.
>
> No one would imagine this spit-fire, full of charm, beautiful
> smile of a woman would be huddled in her car last night sobbing
> inconsolably for 4 hours. I then wrote an apology letter to my
> family and friends, but could not come up with a plan that seemed
> least painful.
>
> A gigantic unfulfilled longing to know a true Father's love has
> **caught** me.

Today I find myself still here—on the planet. My eyes are too puffy and red to cry much more . . . and I am so very tired inside. Then I see your first newsletter appear on my iPhone. My inside exhaustion of trying to keep going without being anyone's daughter, is my time bomb. Last night the hope I have been trying to keep seemed to slip away, like the pin taken out of a grenade.

Tired and hopeless I am reading your email and I think, "How does he know the Father so well??" Ed, this may sound dramatic, but I want to know Him more than I want to breathe. HB

Are you ready for the Father you've always wanted?

Father time . . .

Father, I come to You today because I want to know You the same way Your Son does. I am tired of only seeing You through the brokenness of my dad and not being able to connect with You in my life. Father, I have pushed You away so many times, because I don't know who You really are. I am so tired of the broken models that so many men have modeled to me. You sent Your only Son to invite me into Your family. I want to know what it feels like to be completely loved by a Father.

1

A Father's Blessing,
and Why We Need It

I pray that the eyes of your heart may be enlightened
in order that you may know the hope to which he has
called you.

Ephesians 1:18 NIV

The Difference a Father Makes

While speaking recently to a group of football players at a local high school, I asked one of the young athletes, "When you're on the field, do you ever look up into the stands?"

"Sure," he responded.

I asked him, "Who do you look for—and why?"

"I look for my dad," he said, "to see if he's smiling."

Then I asked him, "What does it feel like to see him smiling over you?"

The tough young football player, used to relying on his own strength, seemed to soften. He looked down for a moment, saying, "There's nothing in my life that means more to me than what my dad thinks of me."

Then he looked up at me, a confident smile lighting his face. "When my dad is there watching, there's *nothing* I can't do!"

When God designed you, He had a dream in His heart of what your life would look like. From your first breath, God the Father has sought to reveal to you that He has always been there rooting you on. When you're on the field of life, who are you looking for in the stands? Who is watching you, and whose love empowers you to accomplish everything to which you're called?

Called to Achieve

My young son, Luke, struck out in his first at bat of the city baseball championship. He put his head down and sulked as he walked back to the dugout. Looking for my reaction, he peeked out from underneath his cap, glancing in my direction. I raised my arms in victory and shouted, "You are a champion, son! You are going to blast the next one!"

His countenance changed from a frown to a smile. In his next at bat, he dug in and smacked the first pitch off the centerfield fence. As he rounded second base with a stand-up double, he raised his hands and gave me the victory sign.

My son caught my smile and knew that he was seen and loved by his father. My love made a real difference in his life.

What was your dad like? Did he lower his head, shaking it in disappointment whenever you failed to measure up? Was he absent, or was he there rooting for you no matter what you did?

If you're a dad, what kind of dad are you?

An involved father can make all the difference in a child's life. His love and care can be the deciding factor in helping a young one become who he or she was created to be. When our hearts are filled with security and trust in a dad who is present and loves us, we transition from living *for* our father's approval, and begin to live *from* his approval.

Who has been in the stands of your life?

Longing to Be Seen

Just like that young football player looking for his father in the stands, each of us is longing to be seen. We're all kids who are hungry for the attention of our fathers.

This longing springs from the core of who we are. It goes beyond a simple desire for approval—although we long for that as well, a longing we'll examine further in chapter 4. Our longing to be seen is a desire to know that someone who loves us deeply is watching over us. We were made to be seen, to live our lives in front of others in relationship, and without those first audiences of love, our future is skewed. When our early experiences teach us that we're invisible because Dad never had time to look our way, our later life will be much more difficult.

While writing this book, I missed my youngest son's first week of football practice. The next week I was able to go, and one of the dads who was holding a blocking dummy said something to me that illustrates this. "Man, your son sure brought the heat today—he's a different player this week because you're here." My presence empowered my son to bring the heat. I was the audience he needed.

In human terms, this longing to be seen can never be fully satisfied. Even the best human fathers sometimes fail to be present, and even the purest human love sometimes falters. There are limits to human love, times when we break down or give up. The best human love can give us only a glimpse of God's love—and it is the limitations of conditional human love that compel us to search for something deeper.

Whether we've ever admitted it or not, at the heart of our longing to be seen is a desire to be loved by God. We were made by God to be loved by Him, and even the best earthly love from our dads can't take the place of the perfect love of our heavenly Father. No earthly father can know us *and* love us perfectly at the same time, but that's exactly what God does.

Big Eye in the Sky

It's a scary thing to be completely known, to be seen at all times. But this fear comes from a faulty picture of God. Often we have the image of a God who is displeased with us because we aren't perfect and is constantly watching us in order to catch us doing something bad—yet the opposite is true!

During my time in the NFL, we had a team meeting every Monday to review the film from the previous game. The video was shot by what we called "the big eye in the sky"—the end zone camera that surveyed the whole field. It didn't miss a thing, and our coach loved to hit the reverse button to highlight our mistakes. In one game I blocked the wrong way. My left and right got confused—and luckily the defense thought it was a trick play, allowing our running back to score a touchdown!

As the room darkened and the film came on, I was hoping that the touchdown would hide my mistake. But I knew I was in trouble when the coach said, "Men, I've seen some amazing things in my day, but this next play beats them all." As he rewound and replayed my mistake over and over, my single mistake turned into dozens of mistakes, and my teammates came up with new ways to poke fun at me.

How many of you had a dad who could always point out your mistakes, but who struggled to tell you what he loved about you? That's the way broken fatherhood has been passed down from generation to generation. One broken dad after another, teaching sons and daughters that love is earned by getting it right. Have you heard that? *I'm only hard on you because it's the way I was raised! If it was good enough for me, it should be good enough for you—and I'm only hard on you so that you can be your best!*

Beloved, that isn't the voice of your heavenly Father. God isn't rewinding the film to replay your mistakes in order to teach you a lesson. Instead, His only Son paid for your mistakes on the cross so that you could know what it feels like to be completely loved by His Father.

What picture comes to mind when you think about God looking at you? Do you see Him in the stands encouraging you to take another swing? Or do you want to head back to the bench so that you don't disappoint Him again?

I have good news for you. At the core of the heavenly Father's heart is delight in each one of His children. He knows that no matter how much we try, we have little hope of changing if we don't feel loved. If we're afraid to try because we're afraid to screw up, we'll never change. God's perfect love is the only thing that conquers our fear and restores our hope—it's the only thing that gets us off the bench and swinging for the fences again!

When Luke struck out, my first reaction was to criticize his swing. But what he needed from me wasn't a hitting lesson but a hoping lesson. What he needed in that moment was my smile. Being perfect doesn't make us feel loved—being perfectly loved

23

sets us free to become a new kind of person who lives from the pleasure of God.

The amazing thing is that God, even knowing everything about us, still looks on us with a smile.

Fully Seen, Fully Loved

God wants to set us free from the performance trap. He never bases His love for us on what we do or don't do. It isn't that God will love us *less* if He finally sees the real us—God *already knows* the real us, *and He cannot love us more than He already does*. God longs to smile over our lives and bless us, without waiting for us to measure up or prove our worth.

The love of God the Father calls us into a future with limitless horizons—horizons wider than we can ask or imagine. God the Father has a plan to give us a hope-filled future (Jer. 29:11), a future full of God-led goodness that was prepared before birth (Eph. 2:10). The One who created us and knows the number of hairs on our heads loves us perfectly. In short, God sees us perfectly and loves us perfectly, which makes God the perfect Father.

But how can this be true when we're so screwed up? It isn't that love is blind, because God knows everything we've ever done and will do. No, it isn't that God looks the other way—it's that He looks at us through the finished work of the cross. When Jesus chose to die on the cross, every wrong that would ever be committed was piled onto Him.

Instead of us.

And when Jesus was raised from the dead, we were given the chance to be raised as new creations as well—children of God loved by a perfect Father. For those who know Jesus, God sees us through what His Son accomplished on the cross because of His love for us. God isn't looking for a chance to catch us doing something wrong, because our wrongs have already been taken care of by Jesus. Instead, God is looking for a chance to bless us—to smile at us as we live for Him.

The Last Orphan

All of us long for a father's smile because we live in a world where so many still live as orphans. They don't know what it feels like to be someone's son or daughter apart from the performance of their life.

Countless numbers of us have also grown up without earthly fathers in our lives. We have missed the opportunity to be seen and celebrated by a loving father. Instead, we have grown up alone, in isolation, never watched from the stands by a father who wants us to succeed. Or we have been watched by a father who requires us to earn his approval. Statistics tell us that more than half of the kids in America will go to bed tonight without a father in their home. And countless young people are looking toward the stands, hoping that maybe this will be the day that Dad finally comes.

I coach youth football, and within the first week of practice I can tell the kind of father each of my players has. I can see it in the way they carry themselves and how they relate to other boys. I have kids who are terrified to make a mistake because they are afraid to disappoint their fathers. I can hear the way fathers have spoken to their kids, because it leaks out under pressure. The kids cuss themselves out for not performing—*Stupid! I'm so lame! That was terrible!*—with the voices of their own fathers. How many of us speak to ourselves with the same angry voices of our fathers?

Before church one Sunday, my son Edward packed up his brand-new Nintendo game in a box and said, "Dad, God spoke to me this morning, and asked me to give my game away to a boy in the church who couldn't afford to have one."

I was shocked. This was Edward's favorite new game that he had just opened for Christmas! Also, I was curious about how God spoke to him, so I asked. Edward replied that God shouted at him, *"Edward, give away your Nintendo game!"*

In that moment I heard my own shouting. He'd learned from me that fathers shout at sons. That they demand of their sons. And I heard the lesson drilled into me by my own stepfather, and my football coaches, and other father figures in my life: if you want to get someone's attention, you have to be loud.

In that moment, my heart broke. The tender, loving voice of God inside my son had been distorted by me. It was wonderful that Edward still heard God's voice, and that he was willing to give away his cherished game, but how tragic that he heard his heavenly Father's voice through the filter of his own, broken earthly father.

That helped me understand that what my son needed was the voice of a present, loving father. That's the same thing *all* of us need, and it's exactly what God offers us. The moment we hear *that* voice—that voice of love that speaks tenderly to us without regard for our performance—our days of living in the orphanage are numbered.

Is It Too Late?

Many of us have grown up as spiritual orphans, never knowing the delight that our loving heavenly Father feels toward us. How many of you have grown up with a broken dad or no dad at all and it has affected how you see God in your life? Maybe God has become someone you can't totally trust because your dad was untrustworthy? Or you see God as One who loves you conditionally and is only interested in making sure you never break the rules?

All of us are wounded, in one way or another. None of us has the perfect father, and none of us can be the perfect father, no matter how good we are or how hard we try. Jesus wouldn't have promised us a new Father if we could be perfect as moms and dads!

But there is another reality, a truth deeper than any pain: the Father loves us and He sent His Son to let us know. Through Jesus we can be part of a perfect family, with a Father who is always home, and always watching over us with a smile.

What about the here and now? If we haven't been the fathers our kids need, is it too late? Is there any hope?

At a conference this past year, a ninety-year-old elder of the church was the last one to come forward. With his eyes filled with tears, he told me that his own father never, ever told him that he loved him, and he had not told his own children he loved them. He felt incapable of saying those words because he had never heard them himself, and he assumed that he had nothing his kids could ever want from him.

As we prayed together, the love and blessing of his heavenly Father fell upon this dear old dad. His tears turned to sobs as God's love descended on him. He looked up and said, "I am going to go home, and for the first time I am going to tell my sixty-eight-year-old daughter that I love her."

He did. He told her all of the things he had longed for his own father to tell him. And that relationship was transformed forever.

Beloved, it is *never* too late for God.

Do you believe this? That it's never too late to see a miracle in your heart and in your own family? Let me say it again: *The last word is always hope.* It is never too late to trade in those old wounds for the Father's smile all of us need. It only takes one loving father to change the course of generations—and one perfect heavenly Father to begin the process.

Have you felt like an orphan in your story? Do you feel like your own brokenness has been passed down to your kid's story? I did! I wish I could say that my early years as a father were stellar, but they weren't. Take heart, Beloved. There is never a time when we cannot call on the name of our heavenly Father, never a time when His delight in us fades. God our Father longs to call us into a place of perfect safety and love—a place where we are seen and loved for who we are no matter what we do.

It is from *this* place of blessing that we are equipped to call out our own children into God's good future—a future where it is never too late for us or for our children. Hear this promise in the words of a Celtic Christian blessing:

> *May you drink deeply of God's cup of joy.*
> *May the night bring you quiet.*
> *And when you come to the Father's palace*
> *May His door be open and the welcome warm.*

Beginning Again

Let's begin our journey, now, into the Father's perfect love and blessing. His plan starts with you becoming who the Father meant you to be, and then cemented in His love and blessing, He pours His love and blessing into the children whom you love.

It will take courage to let the Father into those broken places inside you, and to discover how to call your children into godly adulthood. It won't be easy. As God's love walks around the broken places in your heart, there will be pain and difficulty. I know all about this, because the unrelenting love of the Father I have always wanted uncovered my deepest wounds, my false names, my insecurities, and my addiction with myself. I heard someone say, "Jesus loves you too much to leave you the way He found you." I spent so much of my life performing for love. How about you? Are you tired yet? Want a better way? Are you tired of driving your own children on the same performance treadmill that your family introduced to you?

The hope started for me when I met the Father I had always wanted. Are you ready?

Trust me. Your heavenly Father sacrificed His only Son on the cross so He could heal, restore, and release you into a life that's centered on His love and smile for you. That same smile will equip you to transcend the brokenness of your family so that you can become the fathers and mothers God has made you to be. Fathers and mothers who call their own children into a life that unlocks them from their own brokenness and into the life God the Father has meant them to have.

As we catch the smile of the Father for us, His love will bring us home to the place of love and belonging and delight where we were meant to live. And this in turn equips us to be the son or daughter of God that we want our kids to be.

Have courage. The first step on our journey is an examination of what life looks like when it is lived outside the blessing of our earthly fathers and our heavenly Father. It is only when we understand the full reality of orphan life that we can turn toward faithful fatherhood. We can't live beneath God's smile until we face the prospect of life without it.

Are you ready for the Father you've always wanted?

Father time . . .

Father, I give You my story today. The broken one that keeps repeating from my father's house. The one that keeps reminding me that I am broken and forever stuck in what has been done to me. I want a new story for me and my family. I want to know what it feels like to be loved without having to perform for it.

2

The Narrow Horizon
of My Father's House

Not receiving any blessing from your father is an injury
. . . [Our] sense of self-worth, confidence and courage
to take risk is directly proportionate to the support a
father gives.

Robert Bly, poet

Horizons

Blessing plays a pivotal role in our lives. Remember the story I told
in the last chapter about my son hitting a double off the centerfield
wall? When Luke was at a low point, the smile on my face opened
up his heart to try again. It wasn't that my encouragement suddenly produced hand-eye coordination. It was simply that being
there with a smile on my face and an encouraging word gave him
permission to succeed.

Babe Ruth said, "Don't let the fear of striking out keep you from swinging for the fence." How many times have you held back from something that you were called to because you were fearful? How many times have you second-guessed yourself out of a dream? There is a correlation between the way your dad celebrated you and the way you face the challenges of life. If your dad was present and loving, then the sky is the limit. But if you lived with a remote, demanding father, you probably try to fill the stands with your own audience in a futile attempt to feel loved and adored. If you grew up without a father, wouldn't you trade almost everything you've accomplished for a single moment of love and blessing with your dad, a moment in which he told you all the things he loved about you?

That is exactly what our heavenly Father is ready and waiting to give you. The blessing of the Father changes your horizons. The blessing that transfers you out of the brokenness of your father's house, into His Father's house! No longer is life about winning according to the scoreboard of our culture; it's about knowing you are cheered on by the Father who created you. Sadly, most of us miss this, both as children and as parents. Our horizons shrink because we live in fear of failure. This limitation is all too often the curse of living as orphans.

Sons of Reuben

Albert Schweitzer said, "The tragedy of life is what dies inside a man while he lives." Has some good dream or hope died inside of you? Is something dying inside of your children? It is easy for us to be the same kind of dream killer that our past has been to us.

The Bible tells a story about the sons of Reuben that rocked my heart as a father when I read it. After living in slavery in Egypt for generations, the people of Israel had been miraculously saved and delivered by God—only to fall into forty years of wandering in the desert. Finally, the whole nation came to the edge of the Jordan River, and across that ribbon of water was the bountiful land God had promised to give the tribe of Reuben. The sons of Reuben stood looking at a land "flowing with milk and honey"—pretty much everything they'd been dreaming of and longing for during their difficult time in the desert.

This tribe had history here too. Forty years earlier, their fathers had crossed over this same river to scout the land in advance of the Israelites' coming. However, upon seeing the fierce warriors who inhabited it already, all of the spies turned tail and ran. (All except Caleb and Joshua, who knew God's strength would be sufficient to overcome any challenge.) The leadership of the other tribes of Israel, including the tribe of Reuben, missed out on the Promised Land. Their fear held them back, limiting their horizons and keeping them stuck in the limitations of their father's house.

And, of course, it wasn't just the leadership that suffered—those they led suffered too, including the children, with forty more years of desert wandering.

So now, after decades of discipline, Reuben's kids came to that same place of decision that their fathers had faced. You would think they'd be ready to undo the mistakes of their fathers, having learned the hard way the consequences of fear-narrowed horizons. They walked up to Moses, the leader of the whole nation, and said their piece.

"If we have found favor in your sight, let this land," they said, pointing to the less fruitful land on the desert-side of the Jordan River, "be given to your servants for a possession. Do not take us across the Jordan" (Num. 32:5).

Moses couldn't believe his ears. It was like he was talking to their fearful fathers all over again, and that fear was what had gotten the tribes into such trouble. What the Israelites needed to do was unite and cross the river to claim the land God had promised them. Moses asked the sons of Reuben, "Shall your brothers go to the war while you sit here? Why will you discourage the heart of the people of Israel from going over into the land that the LORD has given them? Your fathers did this" (Num. 32:6–8).

Those words jumped off the page and hit me right between the eyes. Reuben's kids learned to live in unbelief and fear, repeating the same actions of their dad. Failed dads, failed kids. In other words, I can hurt my kids' future by the way I live in front of them now. If that's not a wake-up call for dads, nothing is.

How does this story end? The sons of Reuben make a deal with Moses: they would fight the battles along with the other tribes, but they still wanted to settle on the east side of the Jordan, across the river from the Promised Land. So out of guilt they fought, but when the fighting was done, they ran away, satisfied with far less than what God had promised them.

After the wars were over, the prophet Deborah sang a song for each of the tribes, and when she saw the land of Reuben, she sang, "Among the clans of Reuben there were great searchings of heart. Why did you sit still among the sheepfolds, to hear the whistling for the flocks? Among the clans of Reuben there were great searchings of heart" (Judg. 5:15b–16). The sons of Reuben allowed fear to rule them, and so their horizons shrunk to the size of some slightly-better-than-desert pastureland on the wrong side of the river.

The children of Reuben were stuck in their fathers' house of fear, and Moses rebuked them for it when he said, "And behold, you have risen in your fathers' place, a brood of sinful men, to increase still more the fierce anger of the LORD against Israel!" (Num. 32:14).

I was shaken to my own roots when I understood that the way I walk before the Lord transfers right into the futures of my kids' lives. That rebuke carries a promise that our children will also rise up in places of faith, hope, and courage that we live in. That is called our legacy.

What is the legacy that you are transferring to your kids?

Beloved, it is never too late for God the Father to change your story!

Why did Reuben's kids settle for less? It probably won't surprise you to learn that Reuben was wounded by *his* father, just as Reuben's sons were wounded by him. Reuben didn't receive a blessing from his father, and that caused Reuben to second-guess God and live in fear throughout his life. Later in the book we'll look at the settled confidence that is the fruit of being blessed by a loving father—but all too often sons are cursed with fear and a lack of confidence instead.

Blessing your kids helps them answer some of their deepest questions—questions like, "Do I have what it takes to discover all that God has for me?" There is a whole generation growing up with a theme song that says, "If it's going to be, then it's up to me." And left to themselves, they are discovering that fear often has the final word. The wound of living without a father's blessing has created an entire generation of kids raising themselves alone, and they don't even know what's on the other side of the river.

Questions and Answers

It isn't meant to be like this. Our heavenly Father loves us perfectly. His love answers the deepest questions inside our hearts, which allows us to answer those questions for our children. No matter what age we are, from child to parent, we long to know the same things: "Dad, do I have what it takes? What do you really think about me? Do you think I'm beautiful? Am I a man in your eyes? Do you really love me? Do you see me?" The reality is that we simply cannot answer these questions for our sons and daughters until we answer them for ourselves.

When we aren't blessed by our fathers, we struggle to live the life that God has designed us for—a life where we take the focus off ourselves and give away the love that God the Father pours out through His Son Jesus. When we aren't blessed as fathers, we are incapable of passing on God's blessing to our families—the same problem that plagued the tribe of Reuben. Instead, we live as spiritual orphans, and our children do too. Children raised in a home with an absent father, or a father who doesn't know how to bless his kids, live with a brokenness inside them—a longing to no longer be orphaned.

Recently I was riding on an airplane next to a young woman who, right from the beginning of our conversation, proudly boasted in her confident belief that there was no God. It has been said that the first image of what God is like is the kind of father a child has, and many well-known atheists—and hurting Christians too— have written about the pain of their abusive or absent fathers. On this plane, after a two-hour conversation, my seatmate said, "If I would've had a father like you, my life wouldn't be so screwed up."

It wasn't any profound answers I might have spouted that touched that orphan girl's heart. She was simply and profoundly moved by the fact that I was being a present father to her. I wondered if I might have been the first father she had ever really talked to, and I knew that the wound she still carried from her absent father would continue to fester unless she experienced a father's blessing, claiming her true name as a beloved daughter of God. Her horizons would be forever limited, and her questions would remain unanswered.

Changing the Scoreboard

Questions without answers mean that we treat our kids the way we were treated. I lost my own father before I was born, when he died heroically in a plane crash—a story I'll tell in chapter 5. As I was raised by my stepfather, I sensed that I had to live a life worthy of my father's sacrifice. My early attempts at trying to please my father, my stepfather, and my heavenly Father were all about the win-loss column of my life. I didn't think I would be loved or accepted unless I was a winner, unless I was the strongest—unless, unless, unless. Yet no matter how hard I tried, I couldn't win all the time. When I became a father, I drove my kids the same way I'd been driven. Over the course of their lives, I built the same scoreboard that was built for me: love is only exchanged when you win.

We like to think it's natural for a dad to be loving and present and build relationship with his kids. It isn't that fathers don't *want* to do that, but the simple truth is this: *It is almost impossible for a man to give away something he has never received for himself.* And what he *has* received, even if it is absence or abuse, usually becomes the way he fathers his own kids. In other words, how you were shaped, molded, and loved becomes the way of fathering in you.

If we weren't blessed by our dads, we unconsciously use our children to try to bless ourselves and make our lives matter. Have you ever made parenting about you and your needs, and missed a chance to make a difference with your kids? I have! Have you ever manipulated your kids by withholding affection from them in order to "teach them a lesson"? You are teaching them a lesson, but it probably isn't the lesson you intend!

This doesn't only happen with our children, either—any relationship can be a place where our brokenness and narrow horizons cause us to act in fear. Recently I was on my morning walk, praying for my wife and family, when God showed me a broken place in my heart that He wanted to heal. For years I've found it difficult to simply hang out with my wife and not be "doing something productive." My excuse has been that God wired me to focus on the bottom line and get things moving. But God showed me that I had been conditioned to act that way by my stepfather and my coaches, and the cost was the diminishment of emotional intimacy with my wife. I took pride in learning not to be emotional or waste my time on unproductive things. But while I was focused on "doing enough" so that people would see the results and value me, I was missing the fact that my wife—and God!—already loved me for who I was rather than what I was doing.

God's pleasure for you isn't about your performance—it's about your person, and the fact that you are His cherished child. Open your Bible and start reading Galatians 4 if you need proof! Do you see yourself as God's beloved and blessed child? If you don't, it will be nearly impossible for you to give your own children the sort of love that opens their horizons to all that God has in store for them.

False Names

Another consequence of coming from a home without a loving, present father is that we receive false names. The false names that imprison us come from different places, but the result is always the same. Perhaps you were given a false name by your own father. Michael Jackson knew only a critical father who never in his lifetime gave him the approval he craved so desperately. Not far from my office, a beautiful twentysomething model was found murdered and tossed in a trash barrel. She was searching for a man who could heal her wound—the wound from a dad who never knew how to love and bless his daughter.

Perhaps you were given a false name by the father of lies (one of the names of Satan in Scripture), a being who takes perverse pleasure in lying to you about who you are. He is a master in using the brokenness of your parents to keep the blessing of the Father from your life. He knows that if he can keep you stuck in those lies you will never discover who you really are or what it is like to be truly loved by God.

He may have told you that you can never be happy if you follow God, and that you need to be named "independent" if you want to be truly fulfilled. Or maybe your culture named you, and now you think your identity is the same as how good you look, or your weight, or how much money you make. You might have named yourself too, and now your own voice whispers in your head that you're lazy, a failure, or a bad father.

Regardless of where your false names come from, the result is always the same: imprisonment inside a lie. Like a falcon trapped in a cage, we suffer. We weren't made to cower behind our wounds, loneliness, and fear—we were made to soar, held aloft by the breath of the Spirit as our strength is renewed by God. Whenever we accept a false name, our wings are clipped and the bars of our cage become just a little more secure.

Recently I watched a movie that tells the true story of the band *The Five Heartbeats*. There is a scene in which the lead singer's dad says to him, "Son, who do you think you are, trying to be somebody famous? Because I'm s—, then you're s—!"

The son's eyes fill with tears as he walks away, and the mother says, "Why did you talk to your son that way?"

To which the father replies, "You know I love that boy and I just want him to be a better man than I am."[1]

As crude as that example of false names is, I have heard much worse from dads—dads who might feel love, but are prevented by their own brokenness from showing it or making a positive difference with their kids. When we imagine that telling our kids they'll never amount to anything qualifies as love, we can be sure we're held prisoner by more than a few false names.

One of the devil's main goals is to convince you to name yourself by your brokenness. He wants your future horizons to be completely limited by lies. As a matter of fact, the moment that Adam and Eve sinned against God, a spiritual death occurred inside of their hearts as they lost the inheritance of being completely loved by God. Before they sinned against God, their identity came from being born into the Father's house in heaven. No performance for love was needed! No shame existed. "The Father Loves You" was the song of the day. But that changed the day that sin entered the picture. Now all of humankind would be born outside of the Father's house and into human families where our futures would be affected by the kind of dad we had.

The father of lies gained access into our hearts with his lies and deception as we'll see in chapter 4. If the father of lies can keep you naming yourself by your brokenness, you will never discover what it means to really live. But God loves to change broken stories and make the impossible possible! To use Paul's words to the Corinthian church, "Therefore, if anyone is in Christ, the new creation has come: The old has gone, the new is here!" (2 Cor. 5:17 NIV). False names can only hold us captive until we see ourselves as the beloved children of a perfect Father.

Family Fault Lines

When we're trapped in the lies of limited horizons, performance-based love, and false names, it isn't just us who suffer. Our families suffer too. David Blankenhorn, in his book *Fatherless America*, suggests that crime, juvenile delinquency, teen pregnancy, systemic poverty, homelessness, substance abuse, divorce, domestic violence, and virtually every other social ill can be traced back to fatherlessness. "Before [they] reach the age of eighteen, more than half of our nation's children are likely to spend at least a significant portion of their childhood living apart from their fathers. Never before in this country have so many children been voluntarily abandoned by their fathers. . . . Never before have so many children grown up without knowing what it means to have a father."[2] If a loving, present father stabilizes a family, absent and abusive fathers are like fault lines that shake their families to the core.

During my years of ministry to the fatherless, I can't tell you how many men have said to me, "I waited beside my father for days while he was dying, waiting for him to tell me that he loved me." When I ask what happened, the answer is heartbreakingly common. "He never told me."

How will those men model unconditional father-love to their own children? Every son and daughter is wired by God with a need for unconditional love from their fathers. When a son is never loved and blessed by his father, his life shakes and breaks, and he usually perpetuates the brokenness when he starts his own family. When a daughter is never loved and blessed by her father, she has little choice but to believe the lies her false names tell about her. When a father never loves and blesses his children, he widens a fault line of pain that continues for generation after generation.

Who's Your Daddy?

Four young boys were bragging about their dads. "My dad is a doctor, and he's on call every night," said the first.

"Well, my dad is a lawyer," responded the second, "and he travels half the month."

The third boy piped up. "That's nothing—my dad is a scientist, and he spends weeks at a time in his lab!"

Then the fourth boy finally spoke. "My dad is just there."

Who do you think won that debate? Yet isn't it true that we often admire, and even imitate, the first three dads? Pretending that we're really thinking of our kids, we work ourselves to the bone, all the time avoiding the necessary hard work of being a present father. Sometimes it's easier to work on business deals than on blessing our children. And the false names we're given when we put work over family—"success," "go-getter," "killer businessman"—can sound sweet to our prideful ears. It's not true that being successful prevents you from being a great dad, but it *is* true that if you get your name from what you do, you'll spend most of your life trying to prove yourself to others, and in the process you'll miss the opportunity to be the present father your children really need.

Have you ever seen the show *Lifestyles of the Rich and Famous*? I was watching an old rerun and noticed something shocking—they never show any kids! According to the show, the houses and the yachts and the cars are the point of life. No real families live in those houses. There are no marks on the walls, like in my house, from my boys' competitions to see who can throw something the farthest. There are no food splatters on the ceiling from the occasional food fights at dinner, and not a single window is duct-taped from a miss-hit golf ball, baseball, or air-soft pellet that ricocheted during the last backyard battle. In our culture, being rich and successful is often defined by the absence of children. It's hard to imagine a more hollow way to live—or a faster way to ensure that the planet will soon be empty!

God's love is meant to be passed from generation to generation. Did you receive it? Are you passing it on? If a Hollywood executive ever wants to make my life into a television series, I pray it will be called *Lifestyles of the Present and Participating,* not *Lifestyles of the Absent and Disengaged.* I'm no critic, but I *know* which one will get higher ratings from my wife and kids and make heaven shout with joy!

Love and Football

Let me illustrate how a father's unconditional love and a child's experience of that love can defeat false names and widen horizons.

Two years ago, my son Lukas asked me a question. "Dad, will you still love me if I don't play football this year?"

I said, "Of course, Lukas—did you think that my love for you depended on you being a football player?"

Luke responded, "Dad, I wanted to make sure that I wasn't disappointing you if I didn't play on the football team."

I said, "Son, I'll love you no matter what you choose. I trust you as a man to hear from God and make your own choices. What do you want to do?"

He said, "I want to play tennis."

This was a new one. But I rolled with it, saying cautiously, "Well, son, I've never seen you play tennis before."

Luke, with a smile beaming on his face, said, "Earlier today I took my brother's tennis racket, tried out for the team—and made it!"

My jaw hit the floor. As I write this, Lukas is one of the top players on his tennis team, and he's having the time of his life. I went outside with him the other day to try to return his 120-mile-per-hour serve, and let's just say I needed a baseball cup for protection. Ouch!

My son Lukas is like so many men and women I have met who feel trapped trying to live up to what they *think* their fathers want. The fact that I didn't know Lukas was interested in tennis taught me something: I wasn't close enough to his heart to know what his dream was. But that's exactly what our job is as fathers. We are called to listen to the heartbeat of our children's dreams, no matter how soft the sound, and call them forward in love toward wide and wonderful horizons.

Did your father do that for you? Do you do that for your children?

What the world needs now is empowered, loving fathers—fathers named by God who love their wives and children, and whose presence in their jobs, churches, and communities makes a positive difference. Can you imagine what the world would look like if every family was blessed by a loving father?

That's God's dream as well. God says that He "will turn the hearts of fathers to their children and the hearts of children to their fathers" (Mal. 4:6). Your heavenly Father loves you and longs to transform your limitations into blessings. Your children are waiting for your blessing. No matter how broken your father filter is, no matter what false names define you, and no matter how wide your family fault line is, it is never too late to be blessed and see your family become everything the Father wants for you.

Are you ready for the Father you've always wanted?

Father time . . .

Father, I give You the limited horizons of my father's house today. I am tired of always seeing myself through what I didn't receive. I give You all the orphan moments that have shaped me to live outside of Your presence. I need You, Father. Are You there? How do I not transfer the hurt to my family anymore, and begin to live out of Your love and blessing? How do I connect with You when I still hurt and feel alone?

3

Never Too Late to Be Blessed

Words kill, words give life; they're either poison or
fruit—you choose.

Proverbs 18:21 Message

A Daughter's Hunger

Here is part of a letter from a daughter who has yearned to know
her father's love:

My father never shared himself with me. One day over 10 years ago,
I sat over lunch with my father and decided to ask him something
from my heart after returning from years on the mission field . . .

"Dad, I want to know you . . . Being all over the world has given
me time to think about what is important. If you were to die, I
would struggle to name ten things I know about you at your funeral.
I know you are a moral man who did the best you could for your
family, but I long to know who you really are. Things that really

made you who you are today. For instance, why did you go to seminary? Who was your first girlfriend? Why and how did you learn carpentry? Why did you adopt Heidi and me when we were two? "I just want to know you, Dad."

Puzzled and slightly bugged, he said he didn't understand. (My sister had asked a similar question of him years ago and he snapped, saying, "You don't need to know that stuff. I only share those things with my wife [our new stepmother], and that is all." I was hoping being abroad for so long, he may have changed his mind.)

I tried to clarify things. I said, "Dad, I know President Clinton, (I even met him) but I don't 'know' him . . . I know things ABOUT him, but I don't know him relationally—his thoughts, feelings and what he cares about.

"Dad, I want to KNOW you, not just things about you."

It became apparent that he still didn't understand or he didn't really know how to do what I was asking. Or worse, maybe he didn't desire a relationship of "knowing" one another . . . Maybe he just didn't want to know me or be involved in my life. Maybe he did not want to be known . . . By me. By anyone. I didn't know. But my attempt to reach out and talk soon felt like he wanted to throw out the conversational ball I had been trying to toss back and forth . . .

His response was quick and solid with a sharpness in his tone. "I know, you always want me to change. I am never good enough for you."

Broken Father Models

Have you ever struggled being a dad? Not knowing what to say? Not being able to love and connect? I have! I can't tell you how many times I have walked into the house saying, "Tonight, I'm going to make it about my kids," only to fail for the umpteenth time.

In my early attempts at being a good father, I thought I needed to coach my kids by the book. I became an expert at pre-game speeches and motivational shouting, but I didn't know how to connect to their hearts in a way that would let me lead them when it really mattered.

Once I was giving one of those speeches to my oldest son, Edward—and he wasn't buying it! He was rolling his eyes, and his body language was silently screaming at me to stop sermonizing, but I couldn't help myself. I *had* to finish the lesson I was trying to teach him because it seemed *so* important to me. Finally Edward summoned enough courage and interrupted me, saying, "Dad, I think it's time to take the offering!"

"*What?!*" I exclaimed. "Son, you are *not* all that! I've had *sandwiches* bigger than you . . ."

That's when it hit me: I was treating my son in the same broken way my stepfather treated me. I was trying to answer questions my son wasn't even asking. Josh McDowell says, "Rules without relationship will lead to rebellion." Sometimes we're so obsessed with making rules and policing our kids for compliance that we miss out on the relationship—and if our kids rebel, *no* amount of rules will bring them back.

It threw me for a loop when I found myself using the same broken models used by my stepdad and by coaches who had pushed me beyond my limits. Those men challenged me to improve, but I was never secure enough to know that they also cared about me—and they never showed me they did, either.

A high school story captures the sort of man—the sort of father—I would become. At the end of my freshman year, the head coach called me into his office and told me I would never play for him on varsity. He said I wasn't fast enough, big enough, or strong enough. He seemed to take great delight in crushing my hopes.

I dedicated that summer to training as hard as I could, and little did my coach know that I would grow more than six inches and put on thirty pounds of muscle. When training camp began, I walked into his office. His look told me that he didn't recognize me, so I said, "Do you remember me, Coach? I'm Ed Tandy McGlasson, and I've come in today to say that you are a jerk for what you said to me, and I'm going across town to play for another high school."

At the time, I thought that moment proved something about me. It did—but I've come to understand that it wasn't about how successful I was. The real lesson was that I was a man willing to pay any price to be successful. That ethic may have worked on the gridiron field, but it wasn't a recipe for success when it came to fatherhood. What my kids needed was a loving, present father to walk beside them through the ups and downs of life, not a father who could have doubled for a high school football coach. A father who was touchable, real, and revealing about who he was on the inside.

When you try to name yourself by your own effort and success, you never arrive. You are never secure and never finished working, because there is always another mountain to climb. This is true in your job, and it is true in your role as a father. When love depends on performance, the bar will continue to be raised—until one day failure is inevitable.

When you make your life about performing, every relational transaction with your kids is about developing them. Challenging their weaknesses. Teaching them to do the same thing you learned to do: *Remember, love is about performance. Intimacy and vulnerability make you weak and allow others to get ahead of you.* I can't tell you how many memorials I have been to where the surviving children with the wound of their fathers still on their hearts say, "I know that my dad loved me, but he never knew how to say it." Is the legacy you want to leave going to come through the love you poured into your kids or through the trophies and accolades of a life of performance?

My dream for my day before the Lord is to hear my kids say, "My dad gave me everything he had. He loved me, blessed me, cried with me, lifted me up, shared his brokenness with me, asked me to pray for him. He introduced me to the Father who gave me the same name my daddy got: Beloved!"

Listen, Beloved, for me to even be able to write these words is a miracle. The brokenness of my family story set me on a course to transfer the same broken relationships to my kids, but the love of the Father that I never had on earth began rewriting the story of my family. Our Abba Father has a pen in His hand, and His love has already begun to rewrite the ending of your story too.

No Fear

My stepfather's father demanded that he overcome every obstacle. When he discovered that my stepdad was afraid of the water, he drove him to a nearby bridge across a river outside Lake Charles, Louisiana. He then pulled my stepdad out of the vehicle and threw him off the bridge. As he tossed his thirteen-year-old son into the rushing river below, he shouted, "I will not have a son who is afraid of the water—sink or swim, die or try, it's up to you to make it." The day my stepdad told me that story, I was glad there weren't any bridges around!

Is it any wonder that my stepfather became a submarine commander—how better to prove to his dad that he wasn't afraid of the water? I wonder whether this story connects with anything in your life. Has your father ever tossed you from a figurative—or literal—bridge? Have you done that to your own kids?

One of the reasons we repeat broken patterns of parenting is that those patterns, no matter how dysfunctional, are the only connection we have with our fathers. If we don't have the good, we'll still cling to the bad and the ugly, because *any* connection is preferable to *no* connection. I've heard too many adults explain away abusive behavior from their fathers, usually because rejecting that abuse would mean rejecting their fathers entirely. Having a dad—even a broken dad—seems better than being an orphan.

Hurt Begets Hurt

Sometimes we make excuses like, "Well, his generation of men didn't openly share their feelings." That may be true, but it does nothing to bring healing to the heart of a boy who is still waiting for the blessing of his father.

Once, while I was driving with my stepfather, I mocked him when he misspoke. I started to say, "Thát's stupid!" . . . but before I could finish the last syllable, his right arm slammed into my stomach and seemed to ricochet off of my backbone. As I fought desperately for breath, he looked at me and said, "Don't *ever* disrespect me, boy! I made you, and I can take you out!"

That was not one of the better moments in my life. And we like to think that we learn from the past. But what do you think happened years later, when I was a father? One day my oldest son, Edward, said to me, "Dad, that was a stupid thing to do!"

Without thinking, I grabbed him and threw him on his bed, screaming, "Don't *ever* talk to me that way again!"

I was shocked by my brutality. Edward, completely terrified, yelled, "I'm going to call the police on you. This is child abuse!"

Did I count to ten before responding? Dial it down a notch? Apologize? What I actually did was yell back, "Yeah? If you do, they won't be able to find you when they come!"

As I walked out of his room, I was shaking because of the violence that had just exploded in my hands and in my words. This was the son I loved with my whole being, yet my tone was cruel and murderous. Have you had similar moments? In the fire of your anger, have you seen the worst of your father spilling out of you in word and deed?

If we're deeply hurt, how can we be healthy enough to give loving correction without wounding and pushing the hearts of our kids away from us? My journey out of my old father's house had to first start with two questions.

First, how did I really see myself as a man, and second, what dream was I projecting upon my kids' lives? Although performance is a part of life, performing for love is the trap that all of us fall into. When you think about your kids and dream about their future, what do you see? Doctor, lawyer, professional athlete, preacher, successful businessman?

How much of your passion toward them comes after the wins in their lives? How much of your identity is linked into the scoreboard of their lives? If I were to ask your kids what their parents loved about them, what would they say?

So how do we transcend our broken histories and performance for love? Our only hope lies in finding a new Father. When the Bible says, "We love because he first loved us" (1 John 4:19), it's telling us that the love of God is powerful enough to change our entire family story. As a matter of fact, the whole world will know we are Christians by the way we love each other. That is our destiny, Beloved! That is the inheritance we receive as we allow the revelation of the Father's love to invade every part of our broken souls. I was able to bless my family when the Father I always wanted changed my story. He increased my capacity to love others the way He loved me.

How open are you to His love? How much time do you give to letting God father you?

Hurt Doesn't Have to Transfer

Have you done things to your kids that you wish you could take back? Has there ever been a time when your kids were so hurt or so distant that you thought reconnection was impossible? I don't say this lightly: it is *never* too late.

It's never too late to heal family fault lines, to break the cycle of absence, to reconnect, and to become a loving, present father—even if your own father seemed to do everything wrong.

Jesus promised that He would not leave us as orphans. When He said this, He was promising that no matter how our lives began, and no matter what kind of dad we had, He would heal the wounds of rejection and abuse and absence we carry from our fathers—wounds we may have already passed on to our own kids. When we feel more like an orphan than a beloved son or daughter, nothing short of adoption into a new family can break the cycle of pain. God is always ready and waiting to adopt us into His family—no matter who we are or what we have done—which is why it is *never* too late.

So what's the next step? You have to bring your hurt to the Father. You don't have to toss your kids from a bridge to deal with their fear. You don't have to scream at them to be heard. And you don't have to make them perform to earn your love. There is a better way. If Jesus's promise is true, then you can move past the broken parts of your family history.

If you're willing to get honest with God and admit that you still carry wounds from your own father or father figures, then the next step—experiencing the heavenly Father's love—could be one of the most liberating moments of your life.

The father of lies will do absolutely anything to keep you trapped in the prison your father built for you. But I'm here to tell you that it's never too late to be blessed or to be a blessing. God has made a way for you and me to begin again—a life-changing encounter with a new Father who says, "I know the plans I have for you . . . plans to give you hope and a future" (Jer. 29:11 NIV).

Stories of Blessing

I want to share with you some amazing stories that give glimpses of what is possible with God. I'm often asked, "Is it too late to make a difference with my kids?" I meet moms and dads who feel like they blew it as parents; moms and dads who'd give anything to have their kids' hearts back and be a part of their story again. I received an email from a father who asked me that question.

> Dear Ed, I am writing this letter to you to ask for some advice with my daughter. I read your book *The Difference a Father Makes*, and I found myself overcome with tears as to why I destroyed my family and our marriage. It has been over fifteen years since I have been able to communicate with my only daughter. My bitter divorce and the years of separation have caused me to ask: Is it ever too late to reach out to my daughter and become a good father?

John (not his real name) included his phone number and asked if I could call him. I called him that morning and we talked about the brokenness he felt and the pain his own father caused by never telling his son he loved him. That wound caused John to keep everyone far enough away that he would never be hurt again—or so he thought.

After we prayed together, I encouraged him to write a letter to see if his daughter would be open to a conversation. I asked him to start the letter with, "Would you help me understand how painful it was for you when I divorced your mom and for me to not be in your life?"

Within hours of his daughter receiving the letter, John received a phone call from an unknown number. His estranged daughter asked, "Daddy, is that you?"

When John said that it was, her tears started drowning out her words. "Did you leave because I was so ugly?"

Those words pierced John's heart, and he said, "No, honey, you weren't the reason that I left. I was a broken man."

She continued, "I thought you divorced Mom because you didn't want me. I don't remember you ever saying that you loved me. You never hugged me, and I thought it was because I was ugly." Through many more sobs and tears the conversation continued and they agreed to have their first meeting in fifteen years.

The reunion happened at a local restaurant. John asked for forgiveness and explained why he had left the marriage. He was terrified his daughter would reject him, but she didn't, and healing began between them.

Soon John was invited over to his daughter's house. When she opened the door, she said, "Dad, I have a surprise for you."

The front door swung wide and there, standing in front of John, were his two grandchildren—kids he had never known about. Not only was he restored to his daughter, but he became the grandfather he was destined to be. His willingness to reach out *one more time* changed history—not only for his only daughter, but for the two grandchildren he is helping to father today. Truly, it is never too late.

This reminds me of a story in the Bible about Jacob, who was able to see his two grandchildren after thinking that his beloved son Joseph had been killed years earlier.

> Just then Jacob noticed Joseph's sons and said, "Who are these?"
> Joseph told his father, "They are my sons whom God gave to me in this place." "Bring them to me," he said, "so I can bless them."
> Israel's eyesight was poor from old age; he was nearly blind. So

Joseph brought them up close. Old Israel kissed and embraced them and then said to Joseph, "I never expected to see your face again, and now God has let me see your children as well!" (Gen. 48:8–11 Message)

Beloved, God the Father loves to restore families. Did you notice the first thing that Jacob did when he saw his grandchildren? He kissed and blessed them. No matter who you are or what you've done, the same can be true of you—starting right now.

It Ain't Over 'til It's Over

The rock star Lenny Kravitz recently shared about his faith and the final weeks of his dad's life. His father, Sy Kravitz, was a non-religious Jewish man who had little to do with his family following a bitter divorce. Before he died, Sy repented of his sins, accepted Christ, and salvaged what he could of his relationship with his two daughters and son Lenny.

As a result, Lenny made this powerful statement: "The last three weeks of his life was the best relationship I had with him. And it canceled out the forty years before."

It was almost two decades before his father's death, in the midst of his woundedness, that Lenny crafted the words to his highest-charting song to date, "It Ain't Over 'til It's Over."

Despite a bestselling record and the popularity of being an international music superstar, he felt lost without the blessing of his father. Twenty years later, those feelings of bitterness and disappointment disappeared when his father asked his children for forgiveness. Sy Kravitz finally caught the vision of what it meant to be a real father, and a real child of our heavenly Father—and Lenny caught it too. When fathers learn the power their words have, they can forever bless and transform the lives of their children.

So many times we hear stories like Lenny's and assume they only happen to other people. Stories like that might be true, but they would never happen to *us*, right? There is always hope. Believe me, I know firsthand! For years I was stuck repeating the patterns that I learned from my stepdad and coaches, and I thought that the best way to love my kids was to *drive* them to greatness instead of loving them there.

Dad, Are You Ready to Bury Me?

Recently, while celebrating our anniversary in Hawaii, I had a conversation with a father named Tom. Two weeks before Hurricane Katrina, his son John made his regular phone call to his mother. Since John moved out, he never had many words for his dad. That night, as Tom heard the phone ring, he answered and started walking toward his wife to give her the phone. That was when he heard his son say, "Hey Dad, can we talk?"

As Tom told me this story, tears began to form in his eyes as he talked about how hard his father had been on him as a boy. He confessed to me that he'd made mistakes as a father, and he was responsible for some of the distance between him and his son John. Through the years, he was a faithful husband and a good breadwinner, but he still longed for something that eludes so many fathers.

"I wanted to be more than a breadwinner," he told me. "I wanted to have a great relationship with my kids, to be part of their story."

I've met countless dads who would give anything to be able to reconnect with their sons and daughters, to hit the reset button on fathering. So often we repeat the broken patterns our dads gave us without noticing until many years have passed. But it doesn't have to be that way.

Tom got to the heart of his story. As he held the phone to his ear, he heard his son John say, "Dad, I don't want to talk to Mom tonight—I want to talk with you."

Before Tom could think or say anything, there came a chilling question: "Dad, are you ready to bury me?"

Tom couldn't believe what he had heard and asked his son to repeat his question.

"Dad, if something happened to me, would you be ready to bury me? Dad, I feel like the Lord has shown me that I'm not going to live very long." Tom's fingers tightened on the phone as his son continued. "I wanted to call and tell you that I love you and want our relationship to be healed."

Over the next hour, Tom and John shared a transformative father-son experience. He told me that he had one of the most healing conversations with his son since he had moved out years earlier. He longed to reconcile and connect with the son he lost because of his own brokenness as a dad. Words of blessing, forgiveness, and love were expressed. And at the end of the conversation, Tom asked a final question. "John, if I'm going to get ready to bury you, can I ask you about your relationship with Jesus?"

John replied right away. "Dad, I recently gave my life back to the Lord, and you won't have to worry about me when I'm gone." Tom knew at that moment that all his deepest prayers had been answered. After lying dormant for so long, hope had suddenly bloomed. That's why he was able to say what came next.

"Son, I'm ready to bury you."

As Tom told me this story in Hawaii, we were watching a spectacular sunset that painted the entire sky in pinks and oranges. After watching the colors deepen and reflect off the surface of the ocean, Tom looked at my wife and me and continued. "Two weeks after that conversation, my son was on his way home when Hurricane

Katrina struck. A large tree was uprooted." Here he paused and took a breath. "It fell on John's car and he was killed instantly."

In the silence that followed, John said something I'll never forget. "God knew that something deep inside me and my son needed to be healed before he took him home to heaven."

This, my friends, is Jesus's promise in action. His love can never ignore us when our address is outside of His Father's house. He knows that it is never too late to come home.

Dads Are Coming Home

More than two thousand years ago, the Hebrew prophet Malachi announced that before the great and coming day of the Lord, the hearts of the fathers would be turned back to their children. I believe that day is now, and that no matter who you are or what you have done, it is never too late for you to make a difference.

Years ago families had a lot of kids, but today kids have a lot of parents. Everyone wants to tell our kids what to do—including us!—but what they really need is relationship, not rules. They need to know that they are loved for who they are, and they need to be inspired to become who they are meant to be.

We are at a crossroads in our culture. More than half of the kids in America today don't have a father in their lives—but God the Father is on the move to finish what His Son promised. He longs for you to receive the love and blessing that most of our dads did not give us, to equip us to be the man or woman of blessing that our families need. I don't quote these facts to guilt you as a dad to rise up and be different. There is no way for our culture to change by our muscle. We have to have an encounter with the only Father who changes our stories. I have been a witness to an amazing move of God the Father who is equipping men and women to be the channels of blessing that this lost generation needs.

So, you might wonder what was next in Tom's story after the death of his son John? Every year Tom travels to Mexico and helps build orphanages that will care for and bless children who are growing up without fathers and mothers. Tom told me that he never feels more alive than when the last brick is laid, and a home has been built for kids who nobody else wants.

That is what the Father in heaven wants for you! He wants to lay the last brick of His love and blessing on your life so that you would know what it is like to be completely loved by the Father just like His Son Jesus was! As the love of God rebuilds our house, He first needs to rebuild the foundation of the way we see and name ourselves.

How you see yourself determines the kind of life you build for your future. When you think about the identity your childhood gave you, what would it be? When you think of the names that your father called you, what comes to mind? There are names that release blessing in us, and there are also names that keep us stuck.

Which place have you been living? In the place of blessing, or second-guessing your future because you are not sure who you really are?

*Are you ready for the Father
you've always wanted?*

Father time . . .

Father, I now see that it is never too late to be blessed by You and it is also never too late to win the heart of my kids back. I also see that I don't have to repeat the broken patterns of my forefathers. I have lived too much of my life as an orphan and not as Your son or daughter. Change my story, God. I want Your story on my life. Will You be my Father? I don't want to be fatherless anymore. Adopt me as Your child. Claim me as Your own.

4

What Did Your Father Name You?

And as her soul was departing (for she was dying), she called his name Ben-oni; but his father called him Benjamin.

Genesis 35:18

Resetting the Future

This verse in Genesis is one of the most powerful promises for every father who has sired a son or daughter. Every dad who finds himself separated from his kids because he blew it as a dad. Every son and daughter who enter adulthood still carrying the wound of their father rather than the blessing they need to live the life that they have been made for.

This single verse is at the end of a story of a man named Jacob, who years earlier tricked his aging father, Isaac, into giving him the blessing by pretending to be the older brother, Esau. Jacob and his mom conspired to steal Esau's blessing, and set a family feud that lasted for years.

Although Jacob outsmarted his brother, his ill-gotten blessing caused him to receive the same kind of treatment from others in his life, until God stepped into Jacob's story and changed his name to Israel. That single moment with God the Father reset his whole future. It brought healing between him and his brother Esau, and also brought the blessing and favor of God upon his entire family.

Jacob (now renamed Israel), was not present when his beloved wife Rachel gave birth to her second son and with her last breath named him Ben-oni, which means "Son-of-my-pain." I remember the first time I read that verse and it struck me how many children are born in sorrow without a present father in their stories. But the story doesn't end there. Jacob renamed him Benjamin, which means "Son-of-my-right-hand."

In a moment, Jacob, who had just received his real blessing when the Father in heaven renamed him Israel, stood in that same place and changed the destiny of Ben-oni by renaming him. And from that moment in history the tribe of the Benjamites would be born. Men who had the place of favor with their fathers, the right hand of favor that would lead them and be a blessing to many generations to come.

Two powerful truths struck me that day when I read this verse. First, every man who has fathered a child can change the name and history of their child's future. The names we give our kids are very powerful. Second, God the Father loves renaming and blessing us even when we have messed up our futures because of the decisions we have made or the family that we have been born into.

The Power in Our Name

What was the name you came away from your childhood with? I am not necessarily talking about the name on your driver's license as much as I am talking about the names that have been spoken over you. In the Middle East, given names, chosen by the parents, have great meaning over the lives of their children. In the West, some parents are sometimes intentional in the naming of their children, but most of the names we know ourselves by are those spoken over us by our fathers and mothers as we grow up.

I have done hundreds of events these past ten years, and one of the questions I ask men is to tell me the names that their fathers used to call them when they were growing up. The top three names I hear from guys are A**hole, Stupid, and Idiot. Names that belittle instead of empower.

What is the name you were called by your dad? Is it similar to the name that you speak over yourself when you blow it, when you don't measure up, when you disappoint someone? I call these false names, and if repeated internally enough, you can live out of that name the rest of your life.

I remember a moment with my stepdad that gave me one of those false names. Let me paint a picture for you . . . It was my senior year in football. We had just beaten a crosstown rival 42–6. We trounced them. And as I was coming off the field, my stepdad said, "Great game, son, but you know, if you would have just made that last block, you would have scored another touchdown."

I felt like I was slapped in the face. The coaches had awarded me the most valuable player of the game that day. I had thought the goal was to win the game, not to play perfectly. I know that my stepdad wasn't trying to be mean. He was just speaking to me the way he was probably spoken to as a kid.

I am telling you that story because it has marked much of my internal struggle as a man trying to navigate the waters of ministry, family, and friends. I can't tell you how many times I have spoken those words over myself when my sermon wasn't perfect, or my fathering missed the mark, and on and on. Get it? So much of the way we speak internally to ourselves is shaped by those who have projected false names over us or the way we have falsely named ourselves.

Receiving the Right Names

What has come to your mind about how you see and have named yourself? Is it a name God gave you, or has someone or something else named you? Every child born is like a blank canvas waiting for the Master's brush to paint His image on us, but because of the fall of Adam and Eve, your true identity was stolen by a different painter—the father of lies. The devil's plan is to keep you from discovering the name that the Father has reserved for you. As a matter of fact, in the book of Revelation a promise is given to each one of us:

> To the one who conquers I will give some of the hidden manna, and I will give him a white stone, with a new name written on the stone that no one knows except the one who receives it. (Rev. 2:17)

Satan might spend all of hell's resources to keep you trapped in false names, but God the Father sent His only Son to make a way for you and me to live under the same smile and blessing that Jesus lived in.

Yet just as you were born into a family with the name of your father, you were designed to carry the name of the heavenly Father.

The transformative good news of the gospel of Jesus is that no matter what family you were born into, when you become a child of God, a new family name is transferred into your bloodline. This name—Child of God—is the entire blessing that Jesus lived in and from. God, speaking to Isaiah, said,

> No more will anyone call you Rejected,
>   and your country will no more be called Ruined.
> You'll be called Hephzibah (My Delight),
>   and your land Beulah (Married),
> Because GOD delights in you
>   and your land will be like a wedding celebration.
> (Isa. 62:4 Message)

Naming is a part of our identity. There is no such thing as a human who lives without a name. If we aren't named by God, we *will* be named by someone or something else. When we are named by God—Friend of God, Beloved Child—our new identity releases us from false names and empowers us to become who we have always wanted to be.

Yet all too often we are named and cursed by a litany of lies against us, and these wounds are often passed from generation to generation. Instead of looking out across the wide horizon of God's providence, we become trapped in personal prisons of false names—and without meaning to, we pass on the same limitations to our families.

The healing of the father wound starts with the healing of our name. Instead of a father who spoke into you and told you that there is nothing impossible for you, we often fall back into the limitations and fear that our dads lived in. And without meaning to, they plant seeds of brokenness in us by calling us the same names that their fathers called them.

Imprisoned by Our Wounds

Once I traveled to Germany to speak at a conference for Lutheran pastors and Catholic priests. On opening night, I was watching the speaker onstage, and I felt like something was missing for him. Have you ever pushed to convince others while remaining unconvinced yourself? That was how the speaker appeared to me.

Later, I met with him and his family, and I said to him, "Pastor, I was watching you stand on the stage, and although you believe in God's power and gifts, you are teaching things that you have never experienced. You believe it for everyone else, but you still desperately want it for yourself."

His head fell back and he let out a loud groan. One of the pastors who was with us thought I had insulted our host and tried to apologize for my insensitivity and lack of decorum toward this pastor, who was a greatly respected leader in the Lutheran church in Germany. But the pastor interrupted his apology, saying, "Let him finish!"

Under my breath I was crying out for God's help, and he gave me a picture. It was a completed train set, with all the tracks, buildings, and switches in place—but the transformer that was meant to power the train set was not plugged into the wall. This dear pastor started crying, and with tears streaming down his face, he said, "My Father was a German soldier and a very hard man. He never once gave me a present. He never had a birthday party for me, and he never told me that he loved me."

The next few moments were extraordinary, as the love of the Father descended upon this faithful man who intellectually believed that God gives people gifts, but who had struggled to experience that for himself because he had never been given any gifts by his own father. He said, "I have waited my whole life to feel the love of the Father."

No matter how hard he worked, and no matter the perfection for which he strived, his own ability to receive from God was hindered because he saw God through the father wound he carried from his childhood—and it was a broken filter.

I watched as waves of the Father's love descended upon this faithful German man. Although he had never been good at expressing his emotions publicly, he found himself so overwhelmed by the Father's love that he couldn't stop hugging and kissing his wife and son. They were laughing and dancing together, and it wasn't even Oktoberfest!

Is There a Father in the House?

So, what was your home like?

Do you come from a home where your dad didn't know how to lovingly affirm and speak blessing into your life because he was held captive by his own question marks: Who am I? Why am I here? Where is the goal line? Why didn't my dad come to my birthday party?

The devil has been trying to expunge every image that represents loving and faithful fathers from our culture. But why is the devil so father-phobic? Because he knows that if he can continue to destroy families, through broken dads, it will keep us from discovering that there is a heavenly Father who can turn the fatherless into a family of His beloved ones.

Understand, Dads: becoming a loving, present dad is expensive. The entire business world is set up and perpetuated by men who have sacrificed their families for the sake of their careers—both inside and outside the church. The road I am calling you to walk takes great sacrifice! It is the road less traveled, but it is the place of the greatest impact a man can make.

The King's Speech

Recently I watched a powerful and emotionally impacting film, *The King's Speech*. It is a story about King George VI of Britain and his rise to the abdicated throne of his older brother Edward VIII. King George VI was named Albert at birth and was repeatedly abused by his nanny. To make matters worse, his father had little or no contact with him as a child. Albert was continually teased by his family and was named the stammering prince. The lack of love from his father and the abuses of his nanny introduced Albert to a world of fear and uncertainty.

The movie opens with Albert trying to give a speech at the close of the Empire Exhibition at Wembley Stadium. It was the largest public radio broadcast at that time. Albert did everything he could to choke out his words, but he was overwhelmed by fits of stammering and left the stage in utter defeat.

Completely embarrassed, Albert connects with a speech therapist, Lionel Logue, who gives himself to unlocking the voice inside of Albert's life. It turns out that the abuse and neglect of his father set the stage for the limitations that Albert thought were unconquerable in his life. Lionel saw the king inside that Albert couldn't, and he gave himself to setting that man free. Upon the 1939 declaration of war with Germany, Albert, who was renamed with his father's name George VI, was given a three-page speech to be read over the radio. With Lionel's help, King George VI stood up and delivered a speech that restored England's hope.

I have seen this story played out so many times in the lives of young people who have been handicapped by lack of fatherly love and blessing in their lives. How many of you feel like Prince Albert? You are coping rather than living, handicapped with fear and uncertainty. Fear is the fruit of an unblessed, orphaned heart. Courage is the by-product of a life that is secure, because blessing has been transferred and the children's birthright is secure in the reassuring, life-building smiles of their fathers.

Can I ask you a question? When you are on your deathbed, in your last moments, what do you want as a legacy? Will your achievements satisfy you without having the heart of your children? I am not against achievements! But to gain the whole world and lose your family is not enough. Your legacy of love is the only thing that lives beyond you. The money you leave behind to your kids will one day be spent, but the love and name you speak into them will go on for generations.

There is *nothing* in this world worth more than the love of your children. In the Sermon on the Mount, Jesus says this about fatherly blessing: "Which of you, if your son asks for bread, will give him a stone? Or if he asks for a fish, will give him a snake? If you, then, though you are evil, know how to give good gifts to your children, how much more will your Father in heaven give good gifts to those who ask him!" (Matt. 7:9–11 NIV).

No matter how great or how broken your dad was, there is so much more that Jesus came to bring us from His Father. Instead of living from your wounds, you can experience being absolutely loved by the Father you have always wanted with the same love that He loved His only Son with.

How many of you now know that you have been limited by false names? I am not saying that your dad was a bad guy. Maybe he was, maybe he wasn't. What I am saying is that there is great power in the names that we receive and speak over ourselves.

I spent much of my young adult life trying to outpace the limitations of my story. I never stopped moving ahead, and I stayed so busy that I didn't have any time to think. I remember being sore from training as an athlete for much of my childhood, moving from one sprint to another. And the only affection I seemed to get

71

from my stepfather was when I won a game. All of the effort, all of the training, all of the early morning runs was for an attaboy or "you're amazing" from my mom and dad.

How about you? Parents are our first audience, and if we are wounded by them, we quickly learn to push our hearts down and perform for every trophy we can display before them in hopes that they will be proud of us. Here's the problem with performing for love: you will only feel it when you are winning. What about when you need mercy and love the most? Those other days when the scoreboard marks you down as a loser?

So how do you get off this never-ending treadmill of performing for your name? Here's a clue to where we are going. You need a name that is not about your achievements but about who you are to your Father in heaven.

Can you see now what happens when we are named by our wounds and not God's blessing?

In God's intended order, the blessing from fathers to children is the way life is supposed to be transferred, and when it isn't, our kids suffer and are handicapped with the same things we experienced. Without the Father's blessing, we may name ourselves Failures, Deadbeats, or Workaholics. Unblessed by the Father, we aren't the only ones who suffer. All of our other relationships do too.

When the pastor I met in Germany tried to live like he was "supposed to," he discovered that he was trying to draw water from a well that was bone-dry. His father had named him "orphan" by his neglect, and he'd taught his son that he wasn't worthy of a party. His distant, harsh father broke the cycle of blessing, and a family fault line formed. Because his own dad was invisible in his life, he personally struggled with telling his own children what he loved about them, just as he struggled to experience the love and blessing of his heavenly Father for himself. Named by his wounds, he had resigned himself to living with his head down under the constant frown of his disapproving father.

It doesn't have to stay that way, however—and praise God it didn't!

The Wrong Father

Sadly, the first part of the German pastor's story is not unique. It has been retold in one form or another for thousands of years. While the details are always different, the beginning and ending of the story are the same: fatherless children start and finish in heartache. Children who aren't blessed often become parents who don't bless—who can't bless. Countless fathers live with doubts, self-criticism, and paralyzing questions. When and where did it all go wrong?

Contrary to what you might think, this didn't start with your dad. There's another, older father who spends all of his resources trying to keep us from experiencing the blessing of God. The Bible calls him the "father of lies," and we know him as Satan, the Accuser, or the devil. The day he successfully coerced humanity into making sinful choices was the day humanity began to be named by something other than God.

In the early days of the Garden of Eden, the Bible tells us that God was present and walked with Adam and Eve "in the cool of the day" (Gen. 3:8). They had a relationship that was loving and real. Can you picture it? This was a Dad enjoying His children, just as you have probably done with your own children. No agendas, no expectations—just a parent and child enjoying each other's company in shared respect and honor. In our present state, we can't begin to imagine what it was like to walk with God, but in

73

the Garden of Eden, walking with God was the normal way of life. Their names came through their connection with the love of the Father, Son, and Holy Spirit every day.

In this paradise on earth, there wasn't a laundry list of dos and don'ts required to keep order. Because Adam and Eve were blessed and named by their heavenly Father, they were able to live out of that blessing. Their horizons were as wide as the whole earth. They named the animals, enjoyed each other, tended the garden, reveled in the goodness of God's creation, and fellowshipped every day with their Creator. There was but one rule—Do not eat from the tree of the knowledge of good and evil—and it was on this one rule that the father of lies, Satan, focused his effort.

One day, Eve was near this particular tree, and Satan was right there to greet her. He invited her to taste the fruit, promising that her eyes would be opened to her own power. "Eve, eat this fruit and you won't need anyone to tell you how to live your life. You can make your own choices; you can be *self-sufficient*." In other words, Satan used his lies to undermine the blessing that God had given Eve, replacing that with a false name. Instead of being named Daughter of God, dependent on her perfect heavenly Father, Satan wanted her to take a new name: Self-Sufficient. He wanted her to long for her own power, not God's, for her own wisdom instead of her Father's. The ultimate deception was that the man and woman could play God and not only name themselves, but they could determine their destiny and legacy.

Eve listened to Satan's lies and ate the fruit. She wanted a new name for herself because she believed the father of lies instead of her Father in heaven. Listening to Satan's lies, Eve was tempted to make her own rules and control her own future. Thus it was that Eve's true names began to wither, and her false name supplied by the father of lies began to grow like an obnoxious weed.

You know what? I'm sure I would have done the same thing as Eve—and you would have too. That moment in the garden, God the Father lost His children to the father of lies. That day access to the Trinity of God—the Father, Son, and Holy Spirit—would be lost to humankind. No amount of effort could open that door back into the Father's house. Ultimately all of us lost access to the First Family of God, the Trinity. Everything God does in creation has been done in community. Even the Godhead is eternally connected in love, worship, and adoration. Man was created in relationship to that First Family. His whole being, life, and future was designed to have a daily, active connection to the Trinity of God.

Three relationships were lost because of man's rebellion against God's plan.

First, every human being would be born separated from the love and presence of God the Father in their life. No longer would man have the rudder of the Father's voice, direction, and identity. They would have to navigate life without a compass, with their own hands on the steering wheel of life. We would essentially be born alive to the world but dead to God.

Second, man lost the inheritance of our sonship with God. Ultimately we lost our relationship with the Son of God, who the Bible says created all things and each one of us. We lost the inheritance of being the son and daughter of God. We lost the true identity that we were created for, and we also lost access to the revelation of the love of God because of our sin.

Third, man lost the power of the Holy Spirit that equips and gifts him to live out those God-sized problems that come in life. Miracles that used to come through the Trinity to man now had to come through his own power without God.

The curse initiated by the father of lies had sinister, far-reaching consequences. Because Adam and Eve chose to try to become like gods, they also put in place a standard for measuring winners and losers. No longer would people be accepted solely based on God's inherent love; instead, people would struggle to earn love and approval based on following an increasingly complicated set of rules and regulations. When Adam and Eve tasted the fruit, this lie was born: "You are named by your performance, you are loved by your performance, and you have all the power inside of you to make your life work."

No longer could people simply enjoy God's creation and experience a freedom in relationship with him. Our success would now depend on our ability to perform. How many people do you meet who define themselves by what they do for a living? How many dads are still trying to name themselves by their sons' and daughters' achievements? There is nothing more exhausting for a guy than to never feel as though he has arrived. Perhaps that describes you as well. You might feel as if there has never been a smile over your life, only an endless series of days pushing your rock up a hill—with no summit in sight. That kind of life is punishing and exhausting, and it crushes our God-intended dreams and passions beneath its endless grind.

Performance-based approval is one of Satan's greatest weapons. When we listen to the wrong father—the father of lies—our false names become who we are, and our true names are no longer known. Performance becomes the standard for love, and each time we fail, we believe the lie that God doesn't love us unless we are perfect. We pass this lie on to our families too, demanding that they meet certain standards in order to be worthy of our affection and love.

From your earliest moment, Beloved, the devil has been trying to name you by your brokenness. He has been trying to deceive you into thinking that your performance makes you worthy of love—and your inevitable failure makes you worthy of scorn, blame, and shame.

In the years I have been alive, Jesus has changed so many of my false names. He's taken this broken-down boy—named Good Son, Football Player, Performer—and renamed me Beloved Son. It really is that simple and that far-reaching: all our false names must be exposed in the light of the one true name that God has for each and every one of His children. "Long, long ago, he decided to adopt us into his family through Jesus Christ. (What pleasure he took in planning this!)" (Eph. 1:5 Message).

What is the name that you call yourself? Do you long to be called Beloved Son, Beloved Daughter, instead? In other words, no matter how good or bad your own father was on earth, God the Father has planned all along to adopt you into His family and become the Father you have always wanted.

Stuck in the Prison of Our Fathers

One of my friends, James Ryle, was born to a father who ended up getting in trouble and spending time in prison. James, after being sent to an orphanage with his five brothers and sisters, ended up in prison just like his dad. James had a dramatic encounter with the Lord in prison, eventually entering into the ministry. James felt like he was supposed to connect with his dad, whom he hadn't seen in over twenty years. Here is part of his conversation from his book *Released from the Prison My Father Built*:

"Dad, which prison were you in?"

"I was in the Coffield Unit," he replied, unaware of all that was lingering behind my question. The moment I heard his answer my countenance dropped. It was *not* the same prison unit I had been in. I had thought for sure it was going to be the same, and had envisioned preaching rousing sermons about being in the same prison that your father was in; you know, the old "like father, like son" thing. But none of this mattered now. His answer changed all that. "Which prison were you in?" he then asked me, not knowing how my mind was racing. Somewhat dejected, I replied, "I was in the Ferguson Unit, near Midway, Texas; just down a ways from Huntsville."

My dad's expression changed immediately. He went from being curious to being stunned. His mouth dropped open, and he looked at me in disbelief. Gathering himself, he then said the words that would forever mark my life.

"Dear God, son, I *built* that prison."

"What?" I replied. "What do you mean, you *built* it?"

"They used prison labor to build the Ferguson Unit," Dad answered. "I was the welder on the work crew. I welded the bars when that prison was built."[1]

How many of you are still imprisoned by the wounds from your dad? It is a staggering truth that the way we love our kids will either build bars on their future prison cell or set them free into the adventure that God has designed for them. James's story didn't end there. "As Dad's words hung there in the air, the Lord Jesus spoke to my heart, 'James, I have set you free from a prison your father built. Now I will use you to set others free from prisons their fathers have built. Go home to your friends and tell them what great things I have done.'"

That is the picture of what God the Father is doing around the world. The wound that has imprisoned so many sons and daughters is going to be the very thing that God will use to build His family again, when He turns the hearts of fathers back to their children.

There is only one antidote to the false names, father wounds, and family fault lines in our story. We need an encounter with a new Father. We need the blessing that resides in the heart of our heavenly Father. The dream that He has for each one of us is that we would be like His Son and experience the same love that defined the Father/Son relationship of God and His beloved Son. Nothing short of that will do.

How will the Father do that for us?

Jesus prayed, "I made known to them your name, and I will continue to make it known, that the love with which you have loved me may be in them, and I in them" (John 17:26).

What was the name He made known to them?

"Father."

Are you ready for the Father you've always wanted?

Father time . . .

Here I am again, Father, as I bring my heart to You with all of the false names I have tried to live up to. I know that the only way out of the performance trap in my heart is to have a new Father. You! I didn't know that You could be the Father I never had. I have spent most of my time trying to impress You and missed the relationship that You have wanted to give me. Abba, I give You all of the false names that I thought I needed and I only want the name You have waited to give me. Help me repair those relationships where pain has become a wall between me and my kids, and most of all heal my relationship with You as I have spent so much of my time performing for Your love. Jesus, reveal Your Father's love to me so I can know the Father I have always wanted.

In Jesus' name.

5

The Father
You Always Wanted

I will be a Father to you, and you shall be My sons
and daughters.

2 Corinthians 6:18 NKJV

Father Hunger

In the early days of my oldest son's golf career, as we stood on the course one beautiful, sunny day, one of his teammates walked up to me and said, "Could you be my dad? My dad has never come out to watch me compete. I've watched the way you are with your son—I just wish that I could have had a dad like you."

His words stunned me. I wish I could report that this was an isolated story, but I meet orphans every day whose fathers were so preoccupied with their own stories that they never learned to be part of their kids' stories.

Our world is bursting with boys and girls who are hungry for a loving, present father. No matter how old we are, we never stop needing or wanting a father in our story. God made us to be named and blessed throughout our lives, and when we miss out on that we try to replace that relationship with everything and anything we can.

When I watch the hit show *American Idol*, I see a picture of this unsatisfied father hunger in a generation of young people. The audition phase is incredibly painful because so many of the kids don't have a present father, and the audience and the cameras become a chance to be seen and named. There are certainly talented contestants who go on to record successful albums, but along with them are countless kids who could have bypassed being embarrassed on national television if they'd only had a loving, honest dad.

All of us dream about the future, but only our heavenly Father—and loving, earthly fathers who know they are blessed and loved by God—can help us separate our false dreams from the God-given dreams that give us hope and true life.

The Father Jesus Knew

The life of Jesus reveals the difference between God-given dreams and their false counterparts. At least twice during Jesus's life, His heavenly Father spoke audibly and publicly about His Son, saying, "This is my Son, marked by my love, focus of all my delight" (see 2 Peter 1:17; Matt. 3:17 Message).

There is nothing more powerful for a child than to have his or her dad publicly declare his love and delight. Can you imagine being near Jesus on top of that mountain, or at the river, when the voice of God the Father spoke from the sky? Jesus's life was never the same. There were only two times that the audible voice of the Father was heard in Jesus's time on earth, and both times He spoke was to bless and name His Son. Something happens to us when our fathers declare their love and blessing over us, and Jesus was no exception. To hear from your dad, "This is what I love about my son/daughter" can mark you for the rest of your life.

Could it be that those words "You are my beloved Son, marked by my love . . ." were the ones that Jesus repeated over and over again as He faced the impossible task of restoring every one of us born outside of the Father's house and ultimately giving His life away on the cross?

There is something very powerful about a public blessing from a dad. I believe it is the most powerful moment a man can have on earth. To stand in that place as a father to speak life and love into those God has given you to love.

God the Father's blessing that day secured something very powerful inside Jesus: Sonship over performance. The most powerful and anointed place in Jesus's life was Son—not Evangelist, Apostle, Preacher of preachers, King of Kings, etc. . . . but Son!

Think with me for a moment about your life. What if you spent your remaining days connecting to that truth for you as a beloved son or daughter? Jesus didn't spend His days trying to be a Christian. He spent His days following the leading and voice of His Father in heaven. He knew His mission and gave himself completely for it. But His credibility with His followers came as a Son. His own relationship with His Father made His disciples hungry to learn how to live the same kind of life He did.

As a matter of fact, I believe that the most anointed place on earth for a child is to be someone's son or daughter and then God's beloved son or daughter.

Did you grow up in a home where your dad declared his love for you and his delight in you? How would your life be different today if he had told you, "This is my child, marked by my love, and the focus of my delight"? Would you love more, and risk more, and bless your own family more?

When I first read the words that Jesus heard His Father say in that river, my heart shook. My own dad had never said those words to me. It wasn't that he didn't necessarily know how to say those words; it was that his life was taken before I ever got a chance to hear his voice, feel the scratch of his whiskered cheeks, catch a football that he tossed, or look into his loving eyes.

The Father I Lost

It was a late night for Ed Tandy II and his beloved wife Jeanne on May 28th, 1956. Ed loved to read the Bible before he went to sleep, Jeanne snuggling next to him. As Jeanne looked into the face of her lover and the father of her unborn son, she noticed his countenance change. Ed then reached over to his bedside table, grabbed a red pen, and circled something in his Bible. Startled by the seriousness of his look, Jeanne asked, "Ed, am I going to lose you?"

The wife of a Navy test pilot lives every day with the fear that she might lose her man. She learns that every kiss counts, and every embrace could be the last one.

Shaken out of his thoughts, Ed asked Jeanne, "What makes you say that?"

With a puzzled looked, she responded, "It was just the way your face looked while you were reading your Bible."

Ed didn't say anything in reply, but Jeanne wondered if God had just said something to her husband. Five o'clock came early the next morning. Jeanne rolled over to get her goodbye kiss as

Ed left for work. He took off his dog tags and laid them next to her on their bedside table. Little did she know that this day would change her life forever, and shape the destiny of her unborn son. Did Ed know something that caused him to leave his dog tags behind?

Lieutenant Junior Grade Ed Tandy was a test pilot, trained to push the limits of his Fury-3 fighter jet. During his test flight that morning, as he raced through the air at hundreds of miles per hour, the engine began to overheat, and the oxygen system started to fail. Ed was forced to make a split-second decision: he could eject and save his life—sending the plane tumbling out of control toward the ground—or he could remain in the cockpit and help control the plane's descent. It was Memorial Day weekend, and the Monterey beaches below him were filled with families enjoying the holiday. If he ejected, the plane would hit the sand and explode, and if he stayed with his aircraft, the only unpopulated place to guide it was into the ocean.

"This is November Papa 88, taking it in."

This was the final message he sent back to the control tower. Several seconds later, the radio went silent as his plane smashed into the dark blue waters of Monterey Bay. Reports from the beach confirmed his act of bravery—by turning the plane toward the water, he'd avoided a fiery crash into throngs of sunbathers.

Jeanne was in the kitchen preparing dinner when she heard a car pull up. One last look in the mirror to check her face, and off she moved to give her man their traditional lingering kiss at the front door. But the knock on the door signaled to her that it wasn't Ed, but one of his flying buddies. The pilot's eyes told her everything. He tried his best to not choke on his words. "Jeanne, I'm so sorry to inform you, but Ed crashed his plane and was lost at sea."

What every Navy pilot's wife feared the most had happened. The man of her dreams was now relegated only to her dreams. Remembering her last night with Ed, she looked for his Bible in its usual place, and turned to the words he had read less than twenty-four hours earlier. There, in the middle of the page, was a single word circled in red.

Come.

It was the word Peter heard in answer while Jesus walked toward his fishing boat. A storm was up on the lake, and Peter saw his Master stepping across the surface of the dark, chaotic water. Peter had just been bold enough to say, "If that's really You, Jesus, command me to walk on the water with You."

It really was Jesus, which is why the only thing Peter needed to hear was a single word.

"Come."

That single word has had an amazing impact on my mother's life since the night my dad used a red pen to circle it in his Bible. It's changed my life too.

A Mother's Prayer

After my father's death, my mother went into shock. Ed was the love of her life from the first moment they met at a dinner at my grandfather's house, and the shock of his death caused her to sink into a deep depression. She didn't want to eat and started to lose weight. Her mom and dad took her to the hospital, because they feared that she had given up on living and that her baby—who was me, if you haven't guessed by now!—might be in danger.

The doctor's report confirmed their worst fears. "Jeanne," the doctor said, "I'm sorry to tell you this, but there might be something wrong with your baby. We haven't been able to hear the baby's heartbeat, and we think that the devastation and stress of losing your husband has affected your child."

When my mom heard those words, it shocked her right out of her depression. She stood up and said to the doctors, "I am going to have this baby and he is going to be fine!" Then she grabbed her mother's hand and said, "Walk with me, Mom. Now." It was during that walk that she prayed, "God, if you save my baby, I will give him back to you!" And it was on that very walk that her water broke, she went into labor, and I was born Ed Tandy III, healthy and happy.

One year later my mother met another Naval Academy graduate, Dan McGlasson, and was married to him. She wanted me to have a father, and she was still trying to heal from the loss of her true love. Dan stepped up to the plate to pinch-hit for my father, which shows the kind of character he had to take responsibility for a grieving widow and a son who was not his own. It must have been hard for him to live in the shadow of my father's memory, and even though he tried to be the best husband and dad that he could be, my mom never completely let go of her first husband.

My dad wasn't the only casualty of that plane crash. My stepdad was too, and so was I. Like so many kids who lose a parent at an early age, I spent most of my life trying to prove myself worthy of my dad's sacrifice. Constantly living in someone's shadow can be dark and lonely.

No Fear

Remember when I told you that my stepdad's father threw him off a bridge and into a river to "cure" his fear of water? My stepdad inherited that same brutal parenting style and made it his own. I reacted to that by never letting anyone see when I was hurt or afraid.

I thought that if I always looked like I "had it all together," I would be accepted. For years I bought the lie that a real man is tough, unfeeling, and isn't afraid of anything. This was the performance-based approval we talked about in chapter 2—if I was as strong and tough as my stepdad, he would have to love me, because I'd earned it.

Besides being a *very* effective motivator, my stepfather taught me to play football and coached me. One of the things I admired about him was that he hardly ever missed my football games. Yet his presence at these games wasn't always the best thing for me. Presence is crucial, but it has to be the right sort of presence. At my first practice on my stepdad's youth football team, nobody wanted to play center. He looked at me and said, "You get the job." I thought, *How about a vote?* Not on his team.

That day, he became so frustrated with my fear of being hit by the other players that he stopped practice and said, "Son, I want you to run at me and hit me as hard as you can." I didn't want to. I was afraid I'd get hurt, and I didn't want to hit my father. His voice grew louder and louder, however, and the next thing I knew I was charging toward him. Then came a blow from his right forearm and my lights went out.

The next thing I remember was lying on my back and hearing him say, "Are you all right, son? How many fingers do you see?"

What followed that was the lesson. "Listen to me, son! There is no reason to be afraid. No one out here is as big and strong as me, and if you can take my hit, you can take anyone's hit!" My stepdad was pushing me the way his father had pushed him. Did his fear of water disappear after his own dad threw him into the river, or did he simply decide to never let anyone see it again? How many times have you done the same things to your kids that your dad did to you? And how many of those things are *things that didn't work the first time, when your dad did them to you?*

The reason we keep tossing each other off bridges is that we cannot help but see ourselves the way our dads saw us. That is why it is utterly essential that we have a loving, present father in our lives—because perfect love casts out fear.

We All Need Fathers

Are you still performing for your father? Are you still hiding your fears and weaknesses—at least until they come roaring out of you when you talk to your own kids?

We are made to have a father in our story. As a matter of fact, I think it may be impossible to live a healthy life without a loving father—whether biological or spiritual. A father is more than just a biological participant. He is also the first image of who God might be, our first audience, a counselor, a coach, a protector, and ultimately one who helps us discover the future for which God has made us.

The father wound is most often a wound of absence—emotional as well as physical. If we were designed by God to have a father, then when our father is removed or is absent it can devastate us. The most beautiful tree in the world can be killed by simple neglect. Just as a plant requires active input—sun, nutrient-rich soil, water—so we need the input of a father. Without input, we die inside.

We were made for relationship with our fathers, and no amount of friends replaces a father's presence. The big questions inside us are meant to be answered by our dads, and if our fathers are absent from our story, these questions always linger, no matter how "successful" we are.

Beloved, abandonment kills. And what blesses us is what we began this chapter with—the public declaration of a Father: *You are marked by my love, and the focus of my delight.*

Nothing is more debilitating for a young person than looking into the stands and failing to see anyone cheering. When a dad is not there to love, bless, embrace, encourage, guide, and protect, a child grows up thinking, "I must be invisible. My dad doesn't think I'm worth much, or he would want to spend time with me."

Left alone in anger and rejection, shame becomes a child's friend, which further affirms that he or she is not worth much. Distrusting who they are, young people are then easily picked off by other orphans who offer sex, alcohol, and a plethora of attempts to escape the cave of shame.

Many men I know think that the goal of their relationship with God is forgiveness, but it isn't—it's coming home to the Father's house, the place where the door of eternity is open and the welcome is always warm. This is the place from which we need to parent, the place in which the absences and abuses of our earthly fathers are transformed. Turn the page with me as we begin to discover what I call the "sweet spot" of life, which is a way of living that is filled with confidence and security because we know that we are marked by the heavenly Father's love, and the focus of His delight.

Are you ready for the Father you've always wanted?

Father time . . .

Father, much of my search in life has been about finding a father, and You are the only One who can rebuild my life, turning me into the person You have designed me to be. I see that my main pursuit in life should not just be about forgiveness, but rather being adopted by You, Father, through Your Son, who will lead me home to Your house. I now see that until I come home to my Father's house, I will not be able to rebuild my own. Until I see You smile over me, I won't have that same smile for my kids. I want You to be my Father, and I surrender all of those things that have kept me locked in the prison of my earthly father.

6

No More Orphans

I will not leave you as orphans; I will come to you.

John 14:18

The Promise

I mentioned before that Jesus made a promise that is yet to be fulfilled. When He said, "I will not leave you as orphans," He was making a promise to His disciples, assuring them that they would experience the love of the same Father who had loved Him. Jesus's promise was a new beginning for the disciples, and it is a new beginning for us as well. Jesus won't leave us as orphans, but if you have yet to experience the love of the heavenly Father, this promise is yet to be fulfilled.

So how does God heal our father wounds? There is much written today about the depth of the wound of the father on our lives. We have all of the statistics that we need. But how do I leave the wounds of my dad and become the man or woman that God has destined me to be?

God the Father sent His only Son to open the door to the only Father who can heal the wounds inside us. His finished work on the cross paid for every one of our offenses and sins. If the wound you carry comes from your father, isn't it best healed by the heavenly Father? Jesus does not leave us in brokenness but offers us a way to wholeness. He came bearing the greatest gift: the Father's love we've always wanted.

Seen and Loved

I recently attended my daughter's graduation at UCLA. The real story that night didn't come from the stage or from the speakers but from the stands, where the applause of moms and dads was like a wave that washed down over the thousands of graduates. It touched my heart to see parents make fools of themselves to get the attention of their kids.

My daughter called me on her cell phone and asked, "Daddy, do you see me?"

When I heard that question—that question that every child asks—Jill and I responded by jumping up and down like crazy fans! When my daughter saw us cheering, she started laughing, and the look on her face was something I will never forget. It's the same look that our heavenly Father wants to see on our faces, once we realize He sees us and is cheering for us.

The blessing of our Father's love allowed Jesus to live *from* His Father's love, rather than trying to earn His Father's love. Jesus lived a life that was only possible through the loving gaze and affirming voice of His Father. He lived the way we would have lived if Adam and Eve had walked away from that deadly fruit tree and continued to walk and talk with God. Since that fateful day in the garden, each of us is born a spiritual orphan. And ever since then, the Father, Son, and Holy Spirit are executing a rescue plan to tear down our orphanage and lead us into the Father's house.

Are you ready to enter into your Father's house? Let's start where Jesus is marked by His Father's public blessing at the Jordan River.

The Key to the Front Door

About two thousand years ago, the desert outside of Jerusalem was home to a very strange guy. You probably would have smelled him coming before you saw him, the rank odor of his dirt-crusted body drifting across the sand. When he strode into view, his appearance would have confirmed the smell. Looking like a character from a Discovery Channel survival show, John—called the Baptizer by many people—wore ragged, itchy camel skins and a leather strap, which barely held the whole outfit together. His smile revealed his exotic diet, as uneaten grasshopper parts were probably stuck between his teeth. His scraggly beard had traces of wax from his last honeycomb-crunch sandwich.

He was there to baptize anyone who would listen. He would hold them under the water of the Jordan River and raise them up into a new way of living. His mission was to lead people to repentance, but also to serve as the opening act to the greatest story ever told. John preached, saying,

> I'm baptizing you here in the river, turning your old life in for a kingdom life. The real action comes next: The main character in this drama—compared to him I'm a mere stagehand—will ignite the kingdom life within you, a fire within you, the Holy Spirit within you, changing you from the inside out. He's going to clean house— make a clean sweep of your lives. He'll place everything true in its proper place before God; everything false he'll put out with the trash to be burned. (Matt. 3:11–12 Message)

John had been telling everyone who would listen that he was preparing the way for the real star, the One who was coming to rescue His lost children and bring them back to His heavenly Father. One day, as John preached to his usual crowds beside the river, a different man showed up. John began yelling, "Here he is, God's Passover Lamb! He forgives the sins of the world! This is the man I've been talking about" (John 1:29–30 Message).

As Jesus walked into the Jordan River to be baptized, John protested—"No! *You're* the One who should be baptizing *me!*" But Jesus insisted. So John placed his arms around Jesus and lowered Him into the swirling waters of the Jordan River. Then he lifted Jesus out of the water, and as soon as the water cleared from His eyes, Jesus saw the heavens open up and the Spirit of God, like a dove, descending upon Him.

That's when Jesus—and everyone else gathered at the river that day—heard a voice from heaven, a voice filled with love whose words would echo through the centuries as the final answer to the most profound of human problems. What are we named? For what have we been made? Is there anyone who loves us for who we really are?

The voice of God sounded above the rushing of the river and said, "This is my Son, chosen and marked by my love, delight of my life" (Matt. 3:17 Message).

The Context of Love

The meeting at the river between God the Father, God the Son, and God's Spirit seems like a strange way to talk about love. And it *is* strange, until we truly understand the relationship between the Father, the Son, and the Spirit. We call this relationship the Trinity, and while we can't comprehend *exactly* how God can be

Three-in-One, the loving *relationship* between the Father, Son, and Spirit is understandable—and life-changing.

To communicate the depth of the Father's love, think about when a father tells his young daughter how much he loves her. When he says, "Honey, you know Daddy loves you," what is her context for understanding that statement? It is, in part, the way her father loves her mother. If there is a rich and evident love between Mom and Dad, then the daughter says, "Dad loves me in much the same way he loves Mom. He shows me affection, cares for me, holds my hand, and adores me." The context fills in the blanks for the daughter, and she understands something of how deep her father's love is for her.

But what happens if her parents rarely show affection? What if a parent is absent? Then this little girl looks elsewhere for what love means, and most likely she will come up with a wrong definition of what love is all about. This is why the devil spends so much time trying to destroy marriages. If he can pollute the love between a married couple, he knows that their children will have a difficult time understanding what the love of God is like, and those children will therefore continue to live the broken life of orphans.

When a couple demonstrates their love and delight for each other, that couple's children have a clear context for understanding the meaning of love. And when God the Father says that He loves us, our context for understanding that love is the Trinity.

The Dance of Love

Pastor Tim Keller describes the perfect love of the Father, Son, and Spirit as the "Dance of Love." Before the earth was created, throughout all of history, and into eternity without end, there has been a waltz of love within the Trinity. So when God says He loves

THE FATHER YOU'VE ALWAYS WANTED

us, our context is the way the Father, Son, and Spirit have loved each other for eternity. That's what Jesus meant when He prayed, "Father, I want those you have given me to be with me where I am, and to see my glory, the glory you have given me because you loved me before the creation of the world" (John 17:24 NIV).

Do you see what Jesus was asking His Father to show us? He wanted His Father to show us that He was loved by His Father before the foundation of the world, and that love is the same love He wants us to experience!

This reveals at least three things about God's love. First, His love is eternal; it didn't start when you were born, or when you first did something "good" to earn it. Instead, the Father has always loved you. When Jeremiah was a teenager, the voice of God interrupted his walk with these words: "Before I formed you in the womb I knew you, . . . I appointed you as a prophet to the nations" (Jer. 1:5 NIV). In other words, there has never been a time in history when you have not been on the mind of God. He has always loved you with the same eternal love that is present in the Trinity.

Second, His love has designed you perfectly for your destiny. Because He created you in His love, you cannot be a mistake. Even if your mom and dad conceived you out of wedlock, or your dad took off when you were young, or he was killed in action, or you were told that you never should have been born, there is nothing "mistaken" about your life. Your design came before even your parents' birth. You are perfectly made by God—your ethnic background, your gifts, your physical design, the year in history you were born—all of this has been on the eternal mind of God. From the moment of your first breath, God's love has been pursuing you.

Third, the intensity of God's love toward us is measured by the way the Trinity loves one another, not by our definitions of His love. The Bible says, "The Father loves the Son extravagantly. He turned everything over to him so he could give it away—a lavish distribution of gifts" (John 3:35 Message). That's the same extravagant love that God has for us—that God has *always* had for us, and always will. God's love isn't defined by *our* models of love, but by His perfect model.

So here's the big question. Would you be a different dad or mom right now if you allowed yourself to be loved like that?

That's what happened to me. When I met the Father I always wanted, my heart started to change: "You, being rooted and grounded in love, may have strength to comprehend with all the saints what is the breadth and length and height and depth [of God's love], and to know the love of Christ that surpasses knowledge, that you may be filled with all the fullness of God" (Eph. 3:17–19).

The fullness of God is found in the heavenly Father who blesses you, the Son who saves you, and the Holy Spirit who empowers you to love like He has loved you. That is the only true context in which we can understand God's love, and from which we can love and bless others.

Hearing the Wrong Father

My early years of trying to be a dad were hard. It wasn't that I didn't love my kids—it was that I came out of my childhood needing to prove myself because of the loss of my dad and the broken way my stepfather parented. As a dad, it was much easier for me to say, "I told you so" than to say, "Where does it hurt?" It was even harder to stay present and not push my kids away when they disappointed me.

In chapter 3, I related the time I screamed in anger at my son and tossed him onto his bed. When I walked away from that confrontation, I was shaking and totally disgusted with the way I handled myself. Convicted and ashamed, I cried out, "God, why did I do that? You know that I love my son with all my heart!"

Tears formed in my eyes as the presence of the Lord filled the room. Then the loving voice of the Father spoke to me and said, "You spoke that way because it's the same way you speak to yourself when you're wrong. Ed, you have learned to hear My voice through the broken voice your stepfather spoke to you when he was angry. But that's not the way I speak. If you learn how to hear the Father's voice over you—My loving voice—it will make you the kind of father who makes a difference."

My world was rocked! For the first time in my life, I heard the voice of God the way Jesus heard it: full of approval, and love, and hope. When Jesus was on earth, He said, "I only do what I hear the Father saying to Me." What do you think the tone of that conversation was? I had never heard the gentle, tender voice of my heavenly Father. That day His voice made me weep because His loving truth resonated deep within, penetrating to the very marrow of my soul.

Have you ever seen your life flash before your eyes? The Father showed me the way I was loving—and failing to love—those around me. My heart started breaking when I saw how I had made most of my marriage about me, the way I was driving my kids toward performance, and how hard I was trying to prove myself to everyone around me. I had learned to love that way because my whole identity came from trying to prove myself worthy.

That day my heart finally had a much-needed encounter with a Father who was already running toward me in love.

The Father Who Runs toward You

When you think about God as your Father, what image do you see? One of my favorite pictures of God the Father is the parable of the

Prodigal Son. You've probably heard the story before: the youngest son demands his inheritance, runs off to a far country where he blows all his money on women and booze, and then returns home in shame. However, that's where the story gets exciting, because that's when the father runs to meet his son. I think a better title is the Parable of the Running Father.

To understand the seriousness of the story, you have to know what it meant in that day for the son to ask for his inheritance early. The son was basically saying, "Dad, I want to have my inheritance. I don't want your rules; I want to control my own destiny. I want you to die." Pretty brutal!

The son didn't do well without his father and spent his whole inheritance in wild living. When he began to starve, he headed home to become one of his dad's hired servants, hoping to at least have food and a place to sleep. What that son never expected was to see his father running toward him. The son had rehearsed in his mind the speech he would give, but the love-tackle his father gave him silenced his best attempt to ask for forgiveness. All he heard from his dad was, "Hush, child, I have waited for you to come home and I am so grateful that you are here. You were lost and now you are found."

Is that how you would treat a son of yours who wanted you dead so he could have his inheritance early? To the first-century listeners—and to us—this story is a scandal. How can God run toward a sinner, and how can God be such a different kind of Father?

When Jesus taught His friends to pray, "Our Father in heaven," He was teaching a radical new way of relating to God. The religious leaders rejected Jesus's message of fatherly love because they had spent their entire lives proving themselves by their good works—and here came a carpenter's son claiming that God is a Father who runs toward broken children before they've cleaned up their lives.

You might be asking, "But how can God do that when my life is so broken? How can He receive me when I have shattered so many promises?" God is always able to run to us because every offense that we have done, or could ever do, has already been completely paid for by Jesus on the cross. When we turn toward the Father's house, He runs toward us no matter what we have done or left undone, and an encounter with that love changes us into a new kind of person.

From Tears to Tiaras

In case you think that you have a monopoly on serious sin—which is just a twisted version of feeling pride in your performance, by the way—let me tell you a story about some folks who had every reason to think they'd always be in the dark outside the Father's house . . . until they suddenly looked up and saw the Father sprinting toward them with open arms.

I recently visited the Walter Hoving Home, a faith-based rehabilitation center, to share the blessing of the Father with women involved in prostitution, drugs, alcohol, and abusive situations. These women have been devastated most of their lives at the hands of cruel men, and they entered this program to escape the streets and piece together their shattered hearts.

I wasn't sure what I would find as we drove to Pasadena, California. This was my first time ministering in a women's recovery home. My sweet cousin Jeanne had arranged a special meeting with the director, and she had also brought along tiaras for each of the three dozen women. From the very beginning of our time together, these women poured themselves out to Jesus in gratitude and worship. It reminded me of the woman who fell at the feet of Jesus. She washed His feet with her tears, and wiped them with her hair. When rebuked by the religious people, Jesus said, "Therefore I tell you, her sins, which are many, are forgiven—for she loved much. But he who is forgiven little, loves little" (Luke 7:47).

After worship, I began sharing about the love and blessing of their Father in heaven, and their tears turned to audible sobs as the loving presence of Jesus filled that room. One woman I met didn't have many teeth left in her mouth—she'd pulled most of them out with pliers one night in a drug-induced rampage. She had been beaten, abused, neglected, and was now enslaved to a life of drug addiction. Sadly, her story was far from unique.

Over and over I heard the refrains: *My father left me when I was young; My dad was in prison; My dad was there but never really present.* Many of these women chose to marry broken men, thinking they could fix their husbands, and hoping that they would fill the void of love in their hearts. I saw firsthand that day how damaging it is to a girl to not have a loving father in her life.

After I finished sharing, we asked each girl who had never been blessed by her father to climb to the top of a beautiful walnut staircase. One by one, Jeanne and her team put tiaras on their heads, and I stood at the bottom of the stairs and blessed each girl with the blessing that their fathers would have given them if they had understood God's love. One by one, the affirming power of the Father's words transformed these broken girls into the women God had designed them to be.

To say it was *awesome* would be an understatement. Those were the words of love and blessing these women had been longing for their whole lives, yet no one had ever bothered—or been able—to speak these words to them. What broke my heart that day was the knowledge that I might be the first man in their lives to approach them without selfish intentions, but rather to give them something—the blessing of God the Father—and release them into the healthy adult womanhood that was their destiny in Christ.

Just when we thought we had wiped away the last tear, Jeanne's ministry team stood up and declared, "We want to be blessed too!" These Christian women, who came from influential families in Southern California and looked "great" on the outside, carried the same or similar wounds from their own fathers. Before I could respond, one of the women from the Hoving Home who had just been given a tiara removed it from her head and walked up the stairs and said, "Why don't you take mine?"

One by one, the down-and-out residents of this rehabilitation house proved that their hearts had, indeed, been changed. They had been changed by the blessing of the Father—a blessing that had eluded them their whole lives—and now something deep in their hearts had been transformed, and they were passing that blessing on to others.

It's true that we can't give away what we don't have, but the reverse is true as well. When we *are* blessed by our heavenly Father, we have access to a well of love and blessing that can never run dry.

Receiving Your Blessing

So how do you receive the blessing of the Father?

Let's look again at Jesus's baptism, when His Father declared, "You are My beloved, marked by My love, the focus of My delight." Jesus didn't start His public mission until He was baptized, named, and empowered—and after that audible blessing He began to make a way for every man, woman, and child in history to be welcomed into the Father's house.

Jesus was the most powerful, transformative teacher in history, and His Father spoke to Him audibly only twice in the gospel accounts. We might think that God would back up Jesus's mission by declaring Him to be a prophet, pastor, evangelist, and healer.

Yet what God the Father said to Jesus was that our name is not what we do; our name comes from the revelation of God's love toward us. That is why Jesus was named *Beloved*. His identity was a beloved Son of His heavenly Father, *and every good thing He did in His life depended on that.*

Friend, you are not named by what you have done, or by what has been done to you. Any place can be your Jordan River, the place where you meet your heavenly Father and experience His blessing as He names you.

Being named God's beloved is a model for the way every dad can bless His own children. How many people do you know who feel trapped because they don't know what their own dads think about them? I've never met a wounded person who wouldn't trade *everything* for a great father relationship. God the Father is waiting to give us that great relationship—and when He does, not only will the doors to the orphanage be flung open, but we'll discover that we gave up what we couldn't keep to gain what we can never lose.

God's blessing at the Jordan River wasn't about a single Son. Rather, it was a new beginning for every one of us who longs for that same blessing. Jesus's promise—*"I will not leave you as orphans"*—is being fulfilled. And the only way to leave the orphanage is to be adopted by a new Father.

Could it be that those words from our heavenly Father are a model of the way we are supposed to love our own kids? Could it be that those words over Jesus that day represented the completion of the adoption process that He has planned for each of us? Where the words of the Father you have always wanted repair, renew, and restore you as the spiritual son and daughter you were destined to receive?

What would it mean in your life if you were able to let your own father off the hook of being able to repair, renew, and restore your life? What if your dad is gone or unable to be that kind of father? Are you doomed forever to repeat the same patterns with your kids? With the way you live your life? The way you receive the identity and name God has designed your life for?

Listen to what the apostle Paul told a group of believers. "Long, long ago he decided to adopt us into his family through Jesus Christ. (What pleasure he took in planning this!)" (Eph. 1:5 Message). Do you see God the Father running toward you? He has already hitched up His robes, jumped off the porch, and is sprinting down the road. As His love fills your heart, your gratitude will overflow to those who are still waiting to be blessed.

The Father can't wait to bless you and empower you to be the beloved man or woman you are meant to be.

Are you ready for the Father you've always wanted?

Father time . . .

Father, I am at Your river today to receive life from Your Son, the name You have for me, and the power to live out my days as a godly man or woman. I have spent so many years listening to the wrong father, and I have also been a broken parent to my kids. Forgive me for driving my kids like a coach instead of being a present father or mother with them. Jesus, open my ears to hear the voice of Your Dad and teach me to love and celebrate my kids, the same way Your Father celebrated and loved You.

7

The Trap of Making a Name for Yourself

Then they said, "Come, let us build ourselves a city and a tower with its top in the heavens, and let us make a name for ourselves, lest we be dispersed over the face of the whole earth."

Genesis 11:4

Hey, Rookie

At one time or another you've probably been told, "Go out and make a name for yourself." How's that working out for you? Let me tell you about a time I tried that—and failed miserably.

On my first play in pre-season football for the 1979 New York Jets, my opponent was none other than "Mean Joe" Greene. Yep, my first game-time experience was against one of the most talented defensive lines in history: the so-called Steel Curtain of the

Pittsburgh Steelers—Dwight White, Ernie Holmes, "Mean Joe" Greene, and L. C. Greenwood. We called them the "Black Forest" because they were so massive that the sun was blocked out when they towered over us!

I'd heard that the first hit in the game is the most important, so I went after the 6'7" Joe Greene. I was able to get under his shoulder pads and push him over. I couldn't believe that I had just dominated one of the greatest players in the history of the NFL! I landed on top of Joe—and that's when he said, "Hey, rookie, this is pre-season. Take it easy on me." Joe, like many of the cagey veterans, was just going through the motions, because the real season hadn't started.

However, since I thought this was my chance to make the team, I gave it everything I had. At the end of the quarter, I knew I was facing what might be my last chance to make an impression against this All-Pro noseguard. I broke the huddle and faced the defense, noticing that Joe was acting like a whipped puppy. I snapped the ball to our quarterback Richard Todd and fired off the line to block Joe, but he jumped around me like a cat, grabbed our quarterback, and drove him into the turf like a fencepost. While the crowd groaned, my coach screamed, "McGlasson! You almost got our quarterback killed!"

I knew I was in trouble. As I crept back to our huddle, Joe looked down at me and said, "Hey, rookie—I just wanted you to know who I was."

No matter how hard we try to make a name for ourselves, it can be taken away in an instant. Naming ourselves by what we do can paralyze us when we fail and open the door to false names like Failure and Worthless. There is only one name—the name Beloved, given to us by our Father in heaven—that can define us regardless of circumstances.

The Call

Several years later, I was in training camp with the Philadelphia Eagles when God began to mess with my name. Don't you hate that—when the love of God messes up your "perfect plans" and self-given names? This was the fourth NFL team that I was on. My rookie year 1979 was with the New York Jets, 1980 season with the Los Angeles Rams, 1981 season with the New York Giants, and finally at training camp in 1982 with the Eagles.

I had spent almost every waking hour since I was thirteen working on my plan and dreaming about becoming a professional football player. At training camp, I had one of those sleepless nights—not surprising, given that you wake up each morning wondering if you are going to make it through another day without being cut. Being cut from the team wasn't only about losing my job—it would destroy the name I had made for myself, and it would disappoint all the people who were pulling for me. I thought to myself, *If I'm not Ed the football player, will anyone love or respect me?*

I got restless, so I snuck out of the dorm to spend some time with God. That's when His voice stopped me on my walk and said, "Ed, I want you to leave football and preach the gospel."

Fear instantly grabbed my heart. I thought, *No, not now!*

I had spent so much time trying to prove myself, and I'd *finally* achieved the name Pro-Football Player that I thought would make me, my family, and everyone else happy. When you don't have a dad to name you by his love, it is easy to spend your whole life trying to name yourself by what you do. Pro-Football Player is who I thought I had to be to finally arrive as a man.

I had focused on that dream since I was sixty pounds in Pee-Wee football, and now—at the moment of my success—God wanted me to leave this and be a preacher. The potential of losing my self-name shook me to my core. My entire identity was built around something earthbound, and the love of the Father would not let me stay stuck in the mud . . . but that didn't mean I was ready to change! It wasn't that I didn't *want* to listen to God's call, but *my* plan made more sense to me than God's. I could play football for ten years, amass enough money to care for my family, and *then* I could do ministry work. What was wrong with *that* plan?

Over the years I have watched many of my NFL teammates sacrifice their lives every Sunday in order to give themselves the name their fathers never did. If being famous is the cure to the pain of a fatherless home, why are so many famous people miserable? Even during the writing of this book, another pro-football player was found dead from an apparent suicide. Could it be that our attempts to name ourselves can never satisfy our deepest needs? This latest tragedy is all the more painful because the former player abandoned his only son. One newswriter said, "How can you tell his left-behind son that your daddy loved you and then try to ex-plain why he stuck a gun against his head and pulled the trigger?"

If we listen, there is another voice calling our name, calling us to something that will make a real difference long after we are gone. Unfortunately this voice can be hard to hear, and we're experts at ignoring it.

Just like Your Dad

Being the son of a military hero who died while saving civilian lives contributed to the pressure I felt to achieve. My mom wasn't able to let go of his memory, and there wasn't a day that went by that she didn't say I reminded her of him. Her description of him shaped me profoundly. I wanted more than anything for him to be proud of me and the way that I lived. Being good wasn't good enough—I had to be perfect! This made it almost impossible for me to rest, because I had to get better every day in order to make myself worthy of his sacrifice.

Does that sound familiar? Are you desperate to live up to someone else's expectations or memory, even years or decades after that person has passed on?

When I made the team my rookie year in the NFL, my mom came to see me. "Son, did you know that your father Ed and your stepfather Dan had dreams to play professional football, and now you are fulfilling their dreams?" She meant well, but my mom was putting even more pressure on me—now I had to fulfill my dreams *and* the dreams of my two fathers!

In my story, my absent father was almost *too* good, while in other stories absent fathers are heartbreakingly bad. In either case, what's missing is a father who is both *present* and *loving*. In his fascinating book *Faith of the Fatherless,* social scientist Paul Vitz writes that in his study of the world's most influential atheists—including Friedrich Nietzsche, David Hume, Bertrand Russell, John-Paul Sartre, Albert Camus, and H. G. Wells—all had one thing in common: they had defective relationships with their fathers. When Vitz studied the lives of influential theists—such as Blaise Pascal, Edmund Burke, Moses Mendelssohn, Søren Kierkegaard, G. K. Chesterton, and Dietrich Bonhoeffer—he found that they enjoyed close and loving relationships with their fathers.

Vitz notes that H. G. Wells was contemptuous of both his father and God, writing in his autobiography, "My father was always at cricket, and I think [Mum] realized more and more acutely as the years dragged on without material alleviation, that Our Father and Our Lord, on whom to begin with she had perhaps counted unduly, were also away—playing perhaps at their own sort of cricket in some remote quarter of the starry universe."[1] Media mogul Ted Turner admits his antagonism to God developed after his seventeen-year-old sister died of leukemia and his father committed suicide.

An absent father conditions a child's heart to believe that he or she is alone and unloved. Absent fathers wound hearts, even as they give children broken pictures of what God the Father is like. Who could blame such a child for thinking, *If God the Father is like my father, then I hope God the Father doesn't exist.*

When we have absent fathers, we are forced to make our own names. For some, that name is Influential Atheist. For others, like me, that name is Overachiever and Family Honor-Bearer. I'd finally started to achieve my dreams and make a name for myself, only to have God step in and shatter my self-certainty.

The Call, Continued

Sheer terror filled my heart when the voice of the Father called me away from my own attempts to name myself. The loss of my own father taught me that "if it's going to be, then it's up to me." My early years with my stepdad didn't help this growing ache of feeling alone, since his service in the Navy sent him away for months at a time. I assumed the only person I could count on to take care of me was me.

When God called me out that night, my reaction to His call was fueled by the fear of needing to prove myself all over again. How would I pay for full-time ministry? After seeing the haunting images of televangelists begging for money, I shuddered, thinking about myself in that role. I had the physical skill to be a pro athlete—but being a preacher was uncharted waters.

I think I took the metaphor of uncharted waters too literally. I put all of my money together and tried to build a business that would provide for my family so I wouldn't have to ask anyone for support. I didn't know that the wound I carried from losing my father and the way my stepdad was with money had conditioned me not to trust God for His provision. I went forward on my own, because that was the only thing I knew how to do.

My plan would have earned top honors at the Dumb and Dumber Academy: I started a lobster fishing business. Forrest Gump had it right when he said, "Stupid is as stupid does." I had zero background in commercial fishing, and no particular connection to the sea, yet there I was, ready to motor out into the deep blue and prove that I could provide for myself. My own wife came down to the docks to send me off, shaking her head back and forth, saying, "Ed, I've prayed that God wouldn't kill you for being so dumb."

As I headed out toward Catalina Island off the coast of Los Angeles, California, I had no way of knowing that El Niño that year would devastate the lobster industry around the island. One evening while I was out on my boat, a big storm blew in, and with each towering set of waves, my lobster pots were pushed closer and closer to the cliffs on the back side of the island. I arrived at my fishing area just as the sun was rising, and after eight hours of bone-crushing work, I saw my last three lobster pots near the cliffs in shallow water. I had to time the sets of twenty-foot waves that were roaring in every five minutes; I slipped in with my hook to snatch my last three pots. However, in my tired and frantic state, I didn't notice that the three pot lines had wrapped themselves together. They drifted under my boat and into my spinning propeller. Within seconds, the lines wrapped around my prop and choked my motor to a stop.

Suddenly, I was anchored to the bottom in sixty feet of water with a fresh set of huge waves heading toward me. What happened next seemed like it took forever, but probably lasted mere seconds. The same voice that called me to trust him in Philadelphia now sternly said, "Preach or drown."

113

In other words, His protection and provision would come in what He was calling me to do, not in the things that I was calling myself to do. In that instant, I realized how foolish I was to run from the love and protection of God's calling and put myself in harm's way.

I shouted to the heavens, "Okay, I'll preach the gospel and go anywhere you send me—but save me from this!" I took my boat out of gear and restarted my engine. My attention was drawn to what looked like the biggest wave of the day bearing down on me as I pushed the throttle forward and proclaimed, "In the name of Jesus!" My engine sputtered as my rope-tangled propeller strained for revolutions. All of a sudden I heard a large snap as the prop cut through the ropes. I quickly turned into a huge wave and piloted my little boat up the face of a wave that seemed as tall and steep as a cliff. Did I mention I was screaming at the top of my lungs, "Help me, Lord!"

I barely managed to make it outside the breaking waves, knowing I had to get into the water to finish unfouling my propeller if I wanted to make it back home. I grabbed my Rambo survival knife and jumped into the cold, winter water. Have you ever tried to swim, cry, cut, and repent at the same time? Trust me, it's not easy. The swelling waves and the boat's lurching made it impossible for me to reach the propeller. As I started to fear hypothermia was setting in, I was able to grab the fouled rope with my left hand—and then a badly timed swing with my knife missed the rope and gashed my left hand instead! Blood started pumping out of my hand while the theme of *Jaws* began to play in my head. Afraid of being a main course at a shark dinner party, my paranoia caused every wave to look like a fin. My lips started shaking from the cold and I knew I had only a few moments left. Choking on salt water, I struggled to say, "Help me, God! I don't want to die like this!"

I composed myself enough to attempt a final cut with my knife, and this time I managed to slice through the rope, freeing it from the propeller. However, because of my haste when I jumped off the side, my swim plank was still inside the boat. My climb back into the boat over the jagged edges of the pots shredded my chest. Convinced I was going to die of some ghastly infection, I grabbed the only antiseptic on board—rubbing alcohol—and poured it all over my chest. I let out one of the most powerful primal screams in history . . . that night there was a report on the island that a Sasquatch was heard yowling at sundown!

Still alive, I motored to the harbor and docked my boat. All I could think about was getting to a phone and calling my wife to tell her that I was alive—and finished with my lobster-fishing gig.

Buffaloed

I jumped in my dingy, still wearing my bloodstained T-shirt, and rowed to the main dock so I could call my wife. It was a quarter-mile walk to the telephone, and the wind started picking up. Before I knew it, I was in the midst of a thunderstorm. As I headed toward the phone, I noticed that there was a large herd of buffalo on the road. (The Wrigley family donated parts of Catalina Island to save them from extinction.) My grandfather used to say to me, "Don't buffalo me, Ed." I had no idea what he meant until that day in the middle of a thunderstorm as I stood in front of about three hundred buffalo.

One of the buffalo closest to me started running full speed toward me. I wanted to run away, but my feet were frozen. I stood my ground, and when he got within ten feet of me, he slammed on the brakes and started snorting at me. I thought he looked like the legendary middle linebacker Dick Butkus; my football instincts took over and I started charging at *him*! He ran away, and my path to the phone—and to the rest of my life—was clear.

It wasn't until later that I learned buffaloes are scared of humans, but they charge you to test you and to find out if you are afraid. If you run away, it gives the buffalo courage to keep charging, but if you hold your ground, the buffalo knows who is boss! I could almost see Jesus sitting with His Father on the throne, sending one buffalo after another to teach me a lesson I would never forget.

He is the one who empowers me to fulfill the calling on my life, and if I just stand in front of whatever charges me, He will take care of me. "Therefore take up the whole armor of God, that you may be able to withstand in the evil day, and having done all, to *stand* firm" (Eph. 6:13, emphasis mine).

After I got home from my crazy experience, I sat on the couch with my firstborn in my lap and said, "Okay, Lord, I'm in the ministry."

That was a huge moment in my life. I write about it with laughter now, but it wasn't remotely humorous at the time. Have you ever had an instant of sheer terror when you feel like you're called to do something, yet you have no resources to do it? You're afraid to try, so you attempt to control the situation—or else you live in reckless abandon, making dumb choices and presuming God will bail you out.

My fear drove me to sea, but it took God's love to bring me home. Home was where the love and blessing of the Father was waiting for me, so that I could bless others in turn. God wanted me to live from His love, rather than my own resources, becoming the man that He was calling me to be. If you can relate to this story of being brought to a place where the only option left is to trust, then turn the page and take the next step into the smile of the Father.

Are you ready for the Father you've always wanted?

Father time . . .

Father, it is time for me to come back home to You. There are so many things that You have called me to be, and I can't do them without Your love. I trade in all of my names, trophies, and achievements so I can live the life You have destined me to have. Jesus, open my heart toward further steps to knowing You and Your Father. I want to live the same way You did and know the Father's pleasure over my life.

8

Meeting My Father

> Philip said to him, "Lord, show us the Father, and it
> is enough for us."
>
> John 14:8

The Great Pursuit

The Father is calling you to connect with His love and blessing.
God wants to name and bless you so that you can bless your family.
But is receiving this something you have to do, or is it something
done for you?

C. S. Lewis describes the moment he first came to know the
love of God:

> You must picture me alone in that room in Magdalen, night after
> night, feeling, whenever my mind lifted even for a second from my
> work, the steady, unrelenting approach of Him whom I so earnestly
> desired not to meet. That which I greatly feared had at last come
> upon me. I gave in, and admitted that God was God, and knelt and

prayed: perhaps, that night, the most dejected and reluctant convert in all England. The Prodigal Son at least walked home on his own feet. But who can duly adore that Love which will open the high gates to a prodigal who is brought kicking, struggling, resentful, and darting his eyes in every direction for a chance of escape? . . . The hardness of God is softer than the softness of men, and his compulsion is our liberation.[1]

It was the love of the Father that pursued me when I was afraid. It was the love of the Father that rescued me from the waters off Catalina Island. To understand God's pursuit of us is to understand what His love is about. God is a relentless lover. His choice in loving us was not because of the value that we could add to God's great mission on the earth. No, He chose us in order to love us for eternity—and He chose us before we were even aware of Him!

We humans can understand loving a person who adds value to our life. We often love for the benefits and the perks. It is something entirely different, however, to love someone who cannot add any value to your life. That is a godly love—the kind of love that *gives* the beloved value. That is what the Father's love is like. "But God put his love on the line for us by offering his Son in sacrificial death while we were of no use whatever to him" (Rom. 5:8 Message). In other words, there was nothing about us that deserved to be loved by God, yet God loved us so much anyway that He sent His Son to die for us. God's love is the sort of love that forever pursues the beloved—and the beloved is you!

In my early days of being a Christian, I thought that God did Himself a favor when He saved a professional football player. I was capable and confident, and I could be a witness to Him on the football field. Subconsciously, I thought that God chose to love me because I was lovable and because I deserved it. It wasn't until later that I came to realize the truth: God chose to love me before I ever put on a football helmet—and even before I drew my first breath—and He would keep loving me, even if I left football. The truth is that the Father's love has always been pursuing you. No matter what kind of dad you had, God's love has now come in Christ to give you the same blessing that He gave His only Son. My encounter with that always-pursuing love came in an unlikely place: as I taught a group of high school kids.

The Voice I Needed

A last-minute call came from my youth leader asking me if I could teach his high school group. I jumped in my car and headed for the meeting, thinking about what I would say to our young people. I settled on the classic story of Peter walking on the water, and decided to talk about "Water-Walking Faith."

After we shared a meal together, we entered a time of worship, and then opened the Bible and started reading the story of Peter's water-walking adventure. "And Peter answered him, 'Lord, if it is you, command me to come to you on the water.'" Then Peter receives his answer. "He said, 'Come'" (Matt. 14:28–29).

When I reached the word "come" in the story, the voice of the Father interrupted me. As I stood in front of this crowd of teenagers, all I could hear was the Lord, and He said, "Ed, the last word your father heard before he flew his plane into the sea was the word 'Come.' And that is what I have called you to do. I have called *you* to call *people* to come to *Me*."

I couldn't believe what I had just heard inside of my heart. Despite the sea of young faces watching me, I started weeping. I had wondered my whole life about the way my dad had died, and why God had taken him. I never shared a single moment with my natural father, and it seemed that his life would always remain a mystery to me, sealed and locked. More than anything else, I was simply a son who continued to yearn to hear his father's voice.

That's when God said to me, "Ed, your name is no longer Football Player—you are My beloved son whom I love." In that moment, it suddenly became clear to me that the father I needed—truly needed in the deepest part of my being—wasn't Lieutenant Ed Tandy; it was my heavenly Father. The same voice that spoke to Jesus at the Jordan River opened the horizons of my life and started healing the ache in my heart. The heavenly Father rescued my orphan heart by renaming me with blessing and approval. By receiving the same name and identity that God the Father spoke over Jesus, I finally received the Father's blessing I needed to make my journey as a man complete. Those words gave me the permission and the grace to live out the rest of my life as the man I was called to be.

That moment empowered me to let my dad and stepfather off the hook for my future healing. Even if your dad was able to come absolutely clean with everything he did right or wrong against you, it wouldn't be enough. Why would we need to be adopted by the heavenly Father if our earthly dad was enough? He never will be. I could never be the perfect father that my kids need me to be. As a matter of fact, the biggest part of my job as a dad is to prepare my kids to be adopted by the heavenly Father.

I wish I could tell you that I have been the best father in the world, but I haven't. I have hurt my kids in so many ways. I needed help not only being a better dad, I needed to become a different kind of dad than my stepfather was for me. I needed the father wound inside me healed, so that I would not project and transfer that same kind of wound onto my kids.

The father wound kept me stuck for years waiting for my stepfather or some other father figure to change my story. But all of them ultimately were flawed and couldn't be a perfect father figure in my life. I needed an encounter with the only Father who could change my story. The Father we have always wanted.

The Voice My Kids Need

How often do we misinterpret the desire of our sons and daughters for *identity* as *rebellion*? How many times have we tried to name our kids with rules when they reach the awkward teenage years? When our kids' hormones are raging, it's easy to misread their desire to be named and call it rebellion. We need to set them free and make sure they know we believe in them. We need to bless them. Instead we give them shackles and wonder why they want to break free.

When you were a teenager, what was the question that you wanted your dad to answer about your life?

For me the question was, as John Eldredge puts it, "Dad, do I have what it takes?" That night as I spoke to the high schoolers, the Father I always wanted gave me the blessing that my dad would have given me if his life hadn't ended at four hundred miles an hour.

Those words I heard from God that night mirrored a principle Paul taught: "When I was a child, I spoke like a child, I thought like a child, I reasoned like a child. When I became a man, I gave up childish ways" (1 Cor. 13:11). Two thousand years ago, Paul was saying that becoming a man didn't happen when he reached a certain age—it was released the moment the grace of God empowered him. Whether Paul was blessed by his own father or his heavenly Father, his ability to put off childish things was the fruit of the grace of manhood.

I have met so many wives who are frustrated in their attempts to coerce husbands to rise up and be the fathers they should be. Perhaps those men find it impossible to give away something they have never received. We beat men up over their inability to express their love and blessing for their kids, rather than correcting that inability by connecting them with a Father who can give them the grace they need to be the man, the husband, and the father their families need.

That's what happened to me in front of that youth group. The voice of the Father named me, and the Holy Spirit empowered me to become the man I had been desperately trying to become on my own. My heart's desire for my father's blessing was one of the biggest things I'd been chasing, but I didn't really understand that motivation until I met my heavenly Father. I understood that the Father I always wanted had walked across the water toward my dad's plane that day, and in a single word He had infused my dad with courage *and* spoken a blessing into the next generation.

"Come."

Where are you, Beloved? Are you in a storm? Are you longing to get out of the boat and walk into the manhood and the fatherhood to which you are being called? The Father *is* calling you, and He's waiting for you to listen. It is His blessing that will release the shackles of your family history and free you to walk into the destiny that the blessing of the Father brings. Your children are waiting for you to be blessed so that you can bless them.

Promise Keeper?

Bill McCartney told me that he understood why Promise Keepers struggled to keep the momentum that God had given them. "Ed, we tried to teach men who felt like boys to be promise keepers without understanding that they needed the blessing of the Father first."

Simply *deciding* to act like a man isn't sustainable if you don't have the grace to *be* a man. Being told to "man up" won't last, no matter how noble our intentions. We need to be transformed. And the grace to be a man starts with receiving a blessing from our own dads. That's one reason Jesus came to bring us the Father we have always wanted and needed, even if our own fathers are absent.

Bill went on to say, "If I had it to do all over again, one of the things I would do is to give each man an opportunity to receive the blessing that most of their fathers didn't know how to give them." How many times have you tried to do something with your own power, only to fail and fall short? Our own effort and determination is simply insufficient when it comes to being a godly man year after year.

The Word of God is backed up by all the power of heaven, but something happens in a man's heart when he isn't sure he has what it takes. He limits himself, lives in fear, and holds back. When he is not blessed and named by his own dad, he second-guesses everything he does, and when he tries to "man up" with his wife and kids, he stumbles because he doesn't feel as if he has the grace and power to make a lasting change.

You know what happens next: we hide behind hobbies or lose ourselves in work so that we don't have to come home and hear that we aren't the man she wants or the dad they need.

I'm a broken-down football player who lost his father, but God is using me to broadcast the message of the Father's blessing to every man and woman who longs to be named. This message doesn't flow out of a family history with generations of moms and dads who did it right. This message started in brokenness. Remember, God doesn't use us because we're gold-plated and ready to be displayed to the world. He chooses the humble things of this earth to shame the wise, and He can take any orphaned son and turn him into a godly man, father, and husband.

That's exactly what God did for me, and it was the biggest miracle I've ever witnessed! I humbly offer my life as an example and inspiration: this could be the moment where you and your story are transformed forever. Now . . . are you ready for a swim?

The Blessing at the River

Earlier I talked about the significance of Jesus's baptism in the Jordan River. That wasn't just an important moment for Jesus—it was also a road map to the process by which the Father wants to bless each of us. The blessing of the Father is transformative. After all, if we truly meet our Father in heaven, how could we *not* emerge unchanged?

Jesus was baptized in a river that symbolized the death we are born into. When Adam and Eve chose to disobey God and bite the forbidden fruit, humans experienced a spiritual death that separated us from the love and blessing of our Triune God. That moment of spiritual death caused humans to lose the life-giving relationship with the Son, the blessing of the Father, and the power of the Holy Spirit. When Jesus descended into the cool waters of the Jordan, however, He emerged named and empowered, and we are promised that our future baptism into His name will set us free in the same way.

When the Father's audible voice spoke over Jesus, naming Him the Beloved, it was also the promise of the new name that the Father would bless each of us with in Christ. And the third person of the Trinity, who descended during that moment in the form of a dove, filled Jesus with the power and grace to *be* the Beloved of His Father—to live *from* love instead of trying to *earn* love. God now stands ready to fill you with the power of His grace, through His Holy Spirit, enabling you to do and be everything for which the Father has designed you.

We are saved through the Son, named by the Father, and empowered by God's Spirit to be the sons (daughters), husbands (wives), and fathers (mothers) who can transform the world!

Turning toward Home

Maybe you feel like the son in the Parable of the Running Father, the boy who ran away from home to live it up. Or maybe you're the older son in that same story, who spent his life trying to earn his dad's love by working for it. Either way, neither son understood who his father really was. Earlier in my own story, before I realized my heavenly Father was already running toward me, I had an experience that transformed my perspective.

I had just blown out my knee at football practice my sophomore year in college. The team doctor discovered I had torn my cartilage and three ligaments. The doctor's words in the examining room shattered my dream of playing professional football. He told me there was just no way my knee would ever recover enough to stand up to the abuse of an NFL game.

I went back to my dorm room devastated. The dream I had spent all of my young life trying to fulfill had been crushed by an overzealous teammate diving for the fumble between my legs. The doctors packed my leg in ice, scheduled surgery for the next day, and told me to get some rest. Alone in my room, I began to sob, thinking my life was over because my dream was over. I felt all alone. Worse, I felt like I had disappointed countless people who had believed in me. The uncertainty and fear was overwhelming and I didn't know where to turn.

A few hours later, I heard a knock on my door. I yelled out, "Come in, I can't get out of bed!" Bill Romanowski, the campus pastor whom I had never met, walked in. He explained that he'd heard about my injury. Then he looked me right in the eye and said, "Ed, you have a lot of things going for you, but you lack one thing in your life. Jesus Christ."

I looked at Bill and said, "What is *He* going to do for me *here*?" My leg was in ice, my dream was gone, and now a minister had come into my room to preach to me. The only knowledge of God I had was from movies like *The Ten Commandments*. I thought bad things weren't supposed to happen to me because my dad was a hero. I assumed that God was supposed to keep me from harm because my mom told me He was watching over me. I'd felt like God had saved my life a few times over the years, but now my luck had run out and He'd failed to protect me.

Bill responded by quoting a verse, John 3:16: "For God so loved the world that He gave His only begotten Son, that whosoever believes in Him should not perish but have everlasting life" (NKJV).

When I heard that common verse, my heart understood for the first time that God loved me and gave His only Son to heal my broken life. The Bible says, "So then faith comes by hearing, and hearing by the word of God" (Rom. 10:17 NKJV), and that's exactly what happened to me. With no warning, hearing a Bible verse changed me and filled me with faith. The next thing I knew, I was praying with Bill to receive Christ into my life. I cried as my heart was flooded with the unconditional love of the Father and His Son. I had never felt freely loved like that by anyone before. My questions weren't bouncing off the ceiling—they were reaching the heart of God. I could feel the burden of sin and the guilt begin to lift as the mercy of God washed over my soul and made me new.

It was the first time I felt completely loved for being *me*, not for being a football star. And the logic was as inescapable as it was simple: I could never stop being me, so I would never stop being loved.

Bill then did something that he later told me was out of character for him. He reached out and laid his hand on my ice bag and prayed a simple prayer: "Jesus, heal Ed's knee." I didn't feel anything. My knee was still swollen and numb. But I felt an assurance inside me like I had never had before. I knew God loved me and would never stop caring for me.

The next morning, the trainer came to take me to the hospital. I couldn't feel much in my leg because of the soft cast. They rolled my wheelchair into pre-op and made me put on one of those robes that don't quite close in the back, even on a normal-sized man. After that, they rolled me down the hallway to do an arthrogram: they shot colored dye into my knee to determine what kind of surgery I needed. In those days, they didn't have the arthroscopic technique, so it was slice and dice. After Dr. Michael Vuksta, our team physician, studied the X-rays, he began shaking his head. He looked at me and said, "Here are the X-rays of your knee yesterday, and here they are today. I don't understand it, but somehow all of your ligaments have been reattached. Ed, there is nothing wrong with your knee."

I jumped off of the table to test my knee. It was perfect! I started jumping and dancing while shouting "Hallelujah!"

I couldn't believe what had happened to me. I was a man who had just been healed by God's miraculous love. That was a new horizon. It was hard for me to accept that I could be completely loved by God without working for it—hard to accept that Jesus was the One who paid the price and I no longer had to prove myself. I was conditioned for performance every time I ran out on the football field. I was loved as a victor and booed as a loser. From my first moments with Jesus, however, I saw that He lived life differently than I did. He was filled with joy regardless of whether He seemed to be winning or losing. His motivation was different than anyone I had ever met.

In sports, people like to talk about playing for the "love of the game." I loved the game of football, and for the love of it, I risked everything. What I didn't count on was that football didn't love me back. One way that God brings us to the river to be named and blessed is to expose the insufficient things to which we have given our hearts. That day in college, my knee had been miraculously healed, but I was on notice: football could no longer be the object of my love.

God loved me too much to leave me the way I was.

Training for Something New

Fast-forward several years, and I'll tell you the rest of my story from Eagles training camp. When God called me to leave the NFL, I was *not* ready to listen. The next day while performing a routine pass blocking drill, I planted on my right leg and it buckled under me. Team trainers rushed me to the doctor, who quickly left the room to have a meeting with team personnel. The doctor came back and told me that although I'd injured my knee, it wasn't bad enough to require surgery. They enrolled me in a six-hour-a-day rehabilitation program. Curiously, I could sense an attitude shift with the coaches, who seemed to become more distant. After ten days of rehab, the doctor tested my knee and pronounced me ready for practice. That seemed extremely odd—I'd only been walking in the pool and hadn't run a single step yet.

The next day I reported to the training room. The trainer said, "We're going to tape your knee. We think you're ready to get back out there."

I watched the trainer while he was taping my knee, but he wouldn't look me in the eye. I said, "My knee is still swollen and I can't even run yet."

He just kept taping.

I hobbled out to practice, and during warm-ups I could barely run. I told the coach, and he said, "Don't worry about it. The doctor passed you and I need you to play center." I broke from the huddle and lined up against Charley Johnson, the same player I was blocking when my knee collapsed two weeks earlier. I snapped the ball to the quarterback and tried to push off my knee—only to fall to the ground. I ran another play and my knee collapsed again. The doctor came out, gave me three ice bags, and told me to report to the training room the next morning.

What happened the next day was one of the biggest shocks of my life. Upon reporting to the trainer, I was told to go see team management. I walked into the GM's office, and he said, "Ed, we've decided to release you from the team."

I couldn't believe my ears. I had given my *life* to the NFL—see, I told you I was a slow learner!—and now the NFL was selling me out. "You can't do that," I sputtered. "I'm still hurt and it's against my contract for you to cut me."

They were ready for that. "Listen, Ed," the GM said, "we know you're a good Christian, and that means you won't sue us. And if you try to, I'll make sure you never play football in the NFL again."

My heart was broken. My dream had been stolen from me by a dishonest man. (It later came out that the team owner had a gambling problem and was cutting every possible expense. I happened to be one of those cutbacks.)

Thinking about what he had said, I went home and started to rehabilitate my knee. My wife and I had just welcomed our first son, Edward, and we had very little money in the bank, but I wasn't ready to give up on my dream. Three months later, the Super Bowl–bound Los Angeles Rams called me and asked if I would be interested in joining the team for the playoffs. Excited to have another chance, I showed up for a physical. The team doctor had me run some sprints and asked, "How is your knee feeling?" I could feel that something was wrong, but I tried to hide the pain.

The doctor had me sit on a training table and began to manipulate my knee. "Ed," he said, "it looks like you've torn your cartilage and you need surgery. The Eagles did you wrong."

Without a pass from the doctor, the Rams couldn't pick me up. Worse, even if I never played again, I needed to fix my knee, so I ended up paying for my own surgery, pushing me further into depression and depleting our savings. Giving up my dream to play football was crushingly hard. I now know that God used that moment in my life to transform something deep inside of me—my dependence on something other than Him—but at that time I wondered if God was punishing me because I'd hesitated when He called me to the ministry in Philadelphia.

As I became a man, I had a lot to learn about who the Father really was—and I still do! He isn't petty, and He doesn't punish us just to prove a point. My own projection of God being angry with me and causing my knee to blow out came from my performance mentality. I thought He was disappointed with me because my first reaction was fear. I assumed God was getting ready to toss me off the nearest bridge.

As I entered the ministry, my football career over, I held this same unhealthy mindset. I thought that if my church wasn't growing exponentially, I was a loser. Almost immediately, I found myself trapped in a performance-driven lifestyle, an endless treadmill of never feeling like I had arrived. I knew God loved me, but I still thought it was because of what I did.

Does that sound familiar?

A New Name, a New Way

Jesus lived a counterintuitive life. His greatest joy came by doing the work that His Father sent Him to do. But He didn't do that work to *earn* His Father's love—instead, He delighted in doing His Father's work *because He knew that He was already loved by His Father, simply for who He was.* Jesus was free to fulfill His calling because He was living for the glory of God and was not limited by expectations of the people who surrounded Him.

Have you ever wondered what it would feel like to live without fear? To risk all that you are and all that you have for some greater good that reaches far beyond your own life? What if your service didn't come from your need to prove yourself, but instead flowed out of your sense of being loved by God as His child? Can you imagine a life in which self-promotion and self-focus never had to be part of your day? What if you were able to live like Jesus lived?

That can happen, friend. It truly can. The question is: are you ready for that life?

If you are, turn to the next chapter with me, and let's see what Jesus wants to tell us about His Father.

Are you ready for the Father you've always wanted?

Father time . . .

Jesus, show me Your Father. Open my heart to life, love, and the power of living fully in the smile of His grace. Let me see the glory that You have had since before the beginning of the world. I want to see the manifest love of the Father toward You. I want to live the same way You did—right in the center of Your Father's love over Your life.

9

What Does the Father Think about Me?

He will rejoice over you with gladness; he will quiet you
by his love; he will exult over you with loud singing.

Zephaniah 3:17

A New Father

In the last chapter I showed you that no matter what sort of earthly father you had, or didn't have, your heavenly Father sent His Son so you could have the Father you've always wanted.

The way Jesus walked with His Father is the way *we* are meant to walk with His Father too. When the Father's voice broke through the veil between heaven and earth, the restoration of God's lost family began. The father of lies, the devil, cannot stop God's children from returning to the Father's house and leaving behind their brokenness and false names. When Jesus rose out of the Jordan River, a new family was born, and Jesus (the second Adam) was the first Son of the heavenly Father's new family.

Jesus talked about a day when He would tell us plainly about the Father. I believe that day is now. God is calling His church to become the healthy family He destined us to be, and He is restoring manhood and fatherhood. We see father wounds everywhere we look. So what exactly is our heavenly Father like? To see Him clearly, we must rid ourselves of the broken father filters most of us have carried into adulthood, and look again at the Father as Jesus revealed Him to us. Philip, one of Jesus's disciples, said to Jesus, "Lord, show us the Father," to which Jesus responded, "Whoever has seen me has seen the Father" (John 14:8–9).

Jesus was saying that He was the perfect image of God. He was saying that His actions and words were the very actions and words of God. The religious leaders wanted to kill Jesus, but those who had been following Jesus simply wanted that same kind of life! Like the older son in the Parable of the Running Father, the religious leaders tried to do everything perfectly to earn God's favor. They didn't understand who the Father really was, and they weren't willing to let Jesus show them. Jesus showed us a Father who doesn't love because of performance. He *chose* to love us before we were even born . . . and He can never stop.

In Addition to Love

To understand who the Father is, we need to look at the way Jesus talked about His Father. When Jesus was sharing with His disciples, He said, "It is your Father's good pleasure to give you the kingdom" (Luke 12:32). When you think about the way your dad treated you when you asked for things, what images do you see?

I once asked my stepdad for five dollars, and he looked at me and said, "Five dollars? Do you know how long it takes to make five dollars? I remember when I was your age, I had to walk five miles to school—uphill both ways!" Today I laugh about that story with him, yet I've said similar things to my kids. I learned as a young boy that there was no free lunch, and I had to earn everything. There are still times when I model the stingy heart I received, rather than the generous heart of my new Father in heaven who has given me everything I don't deserve simply because He loves me.

Jesus demonstrated time and again what living from love was all about. He had no problem hanging out with broken people because His identity and mission were secured by the love of His Father. Jesus didn't minister to people to prove He was the Son of God. He loved people because that is what the unconditional love of the Father does. Receiving love from His Father as a Son equipped Him to love anyone His Father brought His way.

We've been talking a lot about love, which can be uncomfortable for some. We know we *need* to be loved, but we *want* to be liked as well. The older son in the Parable of the Running Father wants to be liked, something he tries to earn by his perfect performance. That described me for years. How about you? Like so many older sons, I knew in my head that I was loved, even while I wondered if I'd ever be liked.

Studying the life of Jesus taught me something miraculous: God the Father *likes* me.

That isn't a typo. I didn't mean to write God *loves* me—although He does, for sure! But the Father's love moves Him to *like* us too. So often we're taught that love is a duty, something we do because we have to and not because we want to. There is sometimes truth in that. We all have people in our lives who are hard to love, yet it is our duty to love them anyway. Maybe you have a cranky uncle, or a nosy neighbor, or a rebellious stepson. You don't enjoy loving such people, and most of the time you certainly don't *like* them, but nevertheless you carry on. You take them to appointments, buy them food and clothing, and loan them your lawn mower. You pray for them and treat them with patience and kindness.

But the full truth of the Father is this: it is God's *pleasure* to give you the kingdom. God *likes* you and *delights* in you. Is that the way you approach God and expect Him to move in your life? Or are you hesitant to ask for anything, thinking you need to earn it or that you can't possibly deserve it? Come with me on a short journey as I share three pictures of the Father's pleasure toward you.

His Pleasure in Choosing You

The first picture is a story that is both heartbreaking and heartwarming. The life of baby Corra gives a human face to the never-ending love of our heavenly Father, and shows us how our heavenly Father delights in us—before we do anything to earn it.

Somewhere in California, a young girl was going to become a mother for the first time. Knowing she wouldn't be able to give her daughter the life she deserved, the mother chose a family to adopt her baby. However, when the adoptive parents learned that Corra would be severely handicapped and was likely to die soon after birth, they respectfully withdrew.

The adoption attorney, Ted Youmans, called us and asked us to pray. "Ed and Jill, pray that I'll be able to find a family to adopt Corra. She won't have anyone now to keep her out of harm's way, and she deserves to be loved the same as anyone else."

Adopting a healthy baby is a great way to demonstrate love, but choosing a baby who is severely handicapped and likely to die is an extraordinary kind of love. Ted made a phone call to a couple he knew in Arizona named David and Rebecca. He asked them if they would be interested in adopting Corra. David said, "Ted, you could not have called at a worse time. I'm out of a job and my daughter is starting chemotherapy. But I'll ask my wife and we'll pray about it."

The next day they called Ted back and said, "We want Corra!" David drove to California and discovered the birth mom was in trouble. Losing the first adoptive couple had stung her emotionally, and the hospital was pressuring her to make a decision about Corra's life. She called Ted and said, "David keeps calling the social worker every day. I can't believe he's still interested. I can't believe David and Rebecca still want her with all these problems."

Gradually, the birth mother's heart was transformed. Despite her fears and hurts, she could see the love David and Rebecca had for Corra. One day the call finally came, and David and Rebecca were told that their newest daughter was ready to leave the hospital. They moved little Corra into her new home in Arizona. Welcome cards were taped around her crib and her four new brothers and sisters watched over her while she lay on her soft blankets. Corra had a family who loved her and wanted her.

Six days later, Corra left her broken body and went home to be with the Lord. There hadn't been a single hour of her time on earth when she wasn't surrounded by love.

When I asked David and Rebecca why they endured so much pain and heartache for a child who would likely die soon after birth, David turned the question back on me. "Why *wouldn't* we do that for Corra—she was our daughter!" His answer had nothing to do with what a child can give a parent, and everything to do with the preexisting pleasure a parent takes in their child. That's a perfect picture of our heavenly Father. Instead of being stopped by the cost and heartache of loving us, God looks at us and says, "Why *wouldn't* I love you? You're My child!"

Earthbound love is often about duty or benefits. How many times was your father's love tied to your performance? Was affection withheld when you were at your worst?

What I saw in David and Rebecca was a love that started and ended in delight. It was a love that was not tied down by earthly strings. From the first moment they knew that Corra was their daughter, they delighted in her. When she died, even as their hearts were breaking, they delighted in the time they had shared with her and in knowing she had gone ahead of them to her heavenly Father's home. She didn't have to earn their love and delight. Indeed, she couldn't. But she already had it, and there was nothing she could do to lose it.

Psalm 139 says that God knit you together when you were in your mother's womb. You were perfectly designed by God for what He has called you to be. He delights in the way He made you, and that delight began before you drew your first breath. God likes you. He always has and He always will.

When is the last time you simply *enjoyed* your kids?

When did you last put down the list of the things that frustrate you, or the list of things you need to accomplish, and simply delight in who they are? When did you last *like* them without tying your approval to the person you want them to be? Because of our broken father filters, it's easy to spend time with God and only hear about what we think is broken in our lives. However, there is so much more that God wants to tell you! Did you know God has a dream for you? The apostle Paul prayed for you when he prayed

that the God of our Lord Jesus Christ, the Father of glory, may give you the Spirit of wisdom and of revelation in the knowledge of him, having the eyes of your hearts enlightened, that you may know what is the hope to which he has called you, what are the riches of his glorious inheritance in the saints, and what is the immeasurable greatness of his power toward us who believe, according to the working of his great might that he worked in Christ when he raised him from the dead and seated him at his right hand in the heavenly places, far above all rule and authority and power and dominion, and above every name that is named, not only in this age but also in the one to come. (Eph. 1:17–21)

See the incredible plan the Father has for you! He wants you to know Him. He wants you to know the fullness of His love. He wants you to see why you were made. He has an inheritance for you. He will provide all the power necessary for you to fulfill the mission of your life. He has given you authority in the name of His only Son Jesus. Does that sound like a grumpy Father who requires you to earn everything and whose approval is withheld unless you follow each and every rule?

God's pleasure is to give you His kingdom because He chose to love you before the foundation of the world. Just like David and Rebecca's pleasure was to love little Corra. Even though the pre-birth test showed she would be born handicapped, they chose to adopt her broken body and anticipated short life. God's love enabled them to love her the same way He loves us.

His Pleasure in Watching You

My second picture isn't a tearjerker, but it's just as important in understanding God's delight in you. In his letter to the church in Ephesus, Paul says that each of us was created for good works, which God prepared in advance for us to do. If our heavenly Father delighted in us before we were born, He continues to take delight in us as we live our lives—and part of the reason is that He has prepared great things for us to do.

Think back with me to a story I told in an earlier chapter. My son Luke struck out in his first at bat during a Little League baseball game, and I stood up and yelled, "You are a champion, son! You're going to blast the next one!"

His countenance changed from a frown to a confident smile, and the next time up, he dug his spikes into the dirt of that batter's box, his shoulders squared and ready. Sure enough, he pounded the next pitch, smacking it off the outfield fence for a stand-up double.

Dads tend to be get-it-done kind of guys. We might be tempted to learn the wrong lesson from a story like this. *If encouraging my son means that his batting average will go up, then I'll keep encouraging him so that he's a better player.*

If *that's* our mindset, we're putting more importance on performance than on presence. There's a fine line between demanding performance from someone and widening that person's horizons. What God teaches us is that a Father's delight in His children flows out of the mere fact of His children's existence, *before they've done anything to earn that delight and even after they "mess up" or "underperform."* We may be created by God to do good works, but that doesn't mean God withholds His delight from us until we complete His cosmic checklist.

Look at my son Luke in the batter's box again. In a real sense he was created for good works on the baseball diamond: for line drives, headfirst slides, and diving catches. His body was coordinated and healthy, and his coach made sure he had all the necessary training and practice. Everything that happened before the umpire yelled "Play ball!" was intended to prepare him to succeed at the game of baseball.

So when he struck out his first time up, I didn't stand up and yell encouragement to him just because I thought it might help him get a hit the next time. I stood up because I wanted him to know that I'm in the stands cheering for him no matter what. I wanted him to know that I was his raving fan no matter the score of his life. I encouraged him because I *already* like him—because he is my son—and he hit a double his next at bat partly because my delight widened his horizons. When you rejoice over your kids, it empowers them to accomplish more, because someone they know is rooting for them. I smiled at Luke before he hit his double, and I kept smiling afterward.

That's how it is with God. The main reason we miss His delighted smile is because we've been conditioned to receive smiles only after great achievements. But God smiles over you because you are perfectly created to have relationship with Him. Beloved, when you learn to measure yourself by the depth of His love rather than the length of your résumé, your life will change dramatically. You will begin to feel a growing sense of joy rising in your heart no matter what the scoreboard says. You will understand that God is already delighting in you—right now as you're reading this!—just as He delighted in you yesterday and will delight in you tomorrow.

When my kids feel my pleasure in their lives, it releases them to become what God has made them to be, and it encourages them to live by faith. They know that no matter what they do, their dad likes them. One of my favorite verses in the Old Testament reveals God's heart: "He will rejoice over you with gladness; he will quiet you by his love; he will exult over you with loud singing" (Zeph. 3:17).

Have you ever loved someone so much that you just have to stand up and shout or sing? That's what I did at Luke's baseball game, and that's what the Scriptures say God is doing for *you*. Right now. When your Father in heaven thinks about you, His passion is so great that words are not enough and He bursts into song.

The first time I truly understood this I was in my office at church, watching the online scores of my oldest son Edward's golf match. I wasn't able to make the trip to the Western Open Amateur championships. I missed my son and started thinking about him and all of the things I loved about him. I got so overwhelmed with love for him that I started to dance and twirl around my office. I was on the top floor of my church, and the whole building started shaking as my three-hundred-pound frame leapt across the room. Did I mention I was singing at the top of my lungs? The shaking caused my staff to knock on my door, which I obviously didn't hear. The door opened to the incredulous laughs of my staff watching me perform the Waltz of the Hippo!

I made a fool of myself because of my love for my son. My joy for Edward that day was not because he was playing golf—it was because he was my *son*, and the joy of that knowledge so overwhelmed my heart that I had to sing about it.

As the building finally resettled on its foundations, the Lord spoke to me and said, "As much as you love your son, Ed, you should hear the song that I'm singing over you right now!"

Friend, your heavenly Father is singing over *you* right now, and He sent His only Son to teach you how to hear it.

His Pleasure in Receiving from You

Now, how about a final picture that perfectly illustrates God's delight in you?

Pastor and author John Piper asks, "Do you feel more loved by God because he makes much of you . . . or because you make much of him?" Hidden inside this powerful question is the secret of what it means to be a true son or daughter. The greatest joy children feel is when they bring pleasure to their father. Watching the way Jesus lived in Scripture, we see a Son bringing pleasure to His Father. Jesus said, "I only do what I see the Father doing, I only speak what I hear the Father speaking." He lived the most connected life to a Father that has ever been lived—and He came to show us how to live that same kind of life. Jesus said that His yoke is easy and His burden is light, because we aren't yoked to a plow on earth but to the loving heart of our heavenly Father.

When our identity comes from God, we are set free from the limitations of performing for earthbound crowds. When we lay aside the desire to make a name for ourselves, we start to trust the Father to name us, which sets us free to spend our lives loving the Father we have always wanted.

When I stood in front of those high school kids and heard God speak to me, it changed my heart forever. His voice silenced the orphan heart that ruled my life until I was forty years old. I was no longer invisible and alone on my journey. That voice calls us out of our wounded and limited life and beckons us to the only Father who can make us into something new. That new beginning started the moment Jesus came out of the Jordan River and the audible voice of the Father initiated a new, worldwide family.

Beloved, we are not born again to become a better version of our old selves. God is not "upgrading" us or giving us a few new features. We are born again to become a brand-new creation. A completely different kind of person. When we are born again, the center of our heart can live for the pleasure of our heavenly Father and His bidding, rather than our old idols and selfish distractions. People who give their lives away for the sake of their perfect heavenly Father discover more satisfaction and joy than they ever believed possible . . . and that spills over into their families.

How many Christians still wear the name their earthly fathers gave them? The Father who is waiting to name you is the same Father who named His Son "Beloved"!

Everything in history exists to bring you home to your Father's house. He planned from the beginning of time to one day take the role of the Father in your life. "He predestined us for adoption as sons through Jesus Christ, according to the purpose of his will, to the praise of his glorious grace, with which he has blessed us in the Beloved" (Eph. 1:5–6).

For that moment to be cemented in your life, you must be willing to exchange your old names. You are not named by your family heritage, your ethnic background, the abuse and pain you have suffered, your addictions, your job, your sexual preference, or any other part of your life. No. The only real name by which you will be known forever is the name given to you by your heavenly Father. "You are My beloved son (daughter)." When your name is secure, the smile of the Father becomes the new compass of your heart.

When that happens, every relationship in your life will change. The way you love others—your spouse, your children, even yourself—starts with God, and the pleasure you draw from loving and serving Him will overflow into every part of your life. God loves you, God likes you, and at this very moment God is so delighted with you that He cannot help but sing.

Turn the page with me as we discover how we can give that same smile and blessing away to our kids.

Are you ready for the Father you've always wanted?

Father time . . .

Father, I give You my self-appointed life. I have made much about me because I did not know who You were. I did not know that You were the Father I have always wanted. From the very first moments of my life, You have been pursuing me. You have used everything in my life to point me back to You. Fill my heart again today, so I can make much of You and tell others of the wonders of Your love.

10

The Difference of a Present
Mom and Dad

The Smile That Gives Us Courage

Men, how can you become the fathers that your kids need you to be? Women, how can you become the mother that unlocks the heart of your kids?

This is a key question, and one we're now in a position to answer. The father and mother your kids need is not someone who provides quick answers or always knows what to tell them. No—what your kids need is for you to be close enough to them to matter when things get rough! It's easy for us to get frustrated when our kids are confused. We think that we can power them out of their difficulty and tell them everything they need to know. But at the end of the day, what they need is someone who will not move. A present father is like a wall that our kids can lean against. Someone who is close enough to give them courage because they don't feel alone.

A present mother is also crucial to the destiny of her kids. There is something amazing inside of God's beloved daughters. It is the gift of speaking life into your kids. Telling them all of the things that you love about them. Your power comes through the battles of prayer and speaking more about what you have yet to see in them. You are the relational glue that equips your family to love each other. I couldn't begin to tell you how much my wife, Jill, has taught me about loving my kids. She "gets" them when I don't. God has gifted her to bring His hug to our family.

Mom, you are the one who teaches your kids about how to build intimacy with God. Your tone toward them can either unlock your kids' hearts or drive them away. We don't seem to have as much of a problem with tough love with our kids as we do with being close enough to them to make a difference when they are hurting. Do you want your kids' friends giving them life advice or do you want to be a part of that?

What Do Single Moms Do?

I have many single moms who come up to me at conferences with tears in their eyes as they share about the battles they face without a father for their kids. They are looking for a man somewhere who would help their kids leave the wound of their fathers to become everything they are meant to be.

I have a question for you, single mom. Did God foresee that you would have to raise your kids without your husband? It is not that He didn't want your marriage to work out, but so many guys leave their kids because their fathers did the same thing to them. The shame of doing wrong drives them to run away from being a failure. The father wound inside young fathers drives them to name themselves. Without even being conscious of it, they make everything in their life about them. The casualty so many times is their family. I have met many a successful man in the world's standards who has lost his family to get there.

I know I have been talking about guys here, and there are similarities when girls lose their way as well. Love is not big enough to keep a relationship together, if either one or both is stuck in the wounds of their fathers. That wound imprisons them in the addiction of making life about them. There is always a subtle message behind everything they do. I spent years attempting to get my own way, only to wound the kids whom I loved and the bride the Lord entrusted me with.

So single moms, let me now ask you a question about your family. When your kids watch the way you are doing life with God, would they say that Jesus has been enough for you as a woman and you don't need a man in your life to make your family complete? Would they say that your security as a woman comes from you being the beloved daughter of God, or would they describe you as a wounded warrior who has always been that way? Do your kids hear consistently from you that without a man your life is impossible? Are you projecting your neediness as a woman upon your kids more than the reality that God is enough for you right now? And if He wants to bring you a man to be part of this family, He will have to be an amazing guy. A beloved son, like you are His beloved daughter!

My mom spent many years projecting those same needs upon me as the surviving son of the love of her life, my dad. It was always awkward, because I knew that as her son I wasn't able to meet the needs she needed a present husband for. Parenting is a tough job by itself and losing a spouse through a death or divorce is devastating. But to stay stuck communicates to your kids that God is not enough.

I want you to know that the challenges of being a single mom are overwhelming. Trying to be both parents is not only exhausting for you; it is impossible. I can't begin to understand what you go through. But I say these things to you because I also know that God is bigger than your circumstances and has already preplanned to be the Father your kids have always wanted. Not only your Father, but your kids' Father as well.

I have met some of the most amazing women of faith at my conferences. Girls who have lost almost everything and decided to not project their brokenness upon their kids. I am not saying that they are not lonely for a man in their lives. But they have connected to the love of the Father and connected to Jesus in a way that sows hope into their kids.

The same is true for us guys and the past that we have. We can either live in the brokenness of our natural father's house, or we can transcend that house by receiving the love and blessing that Jesus came to give us access to. When I learned to get out of the way of my kids knowing the Father for themselves, it prepared them to be adopted by the Father for themselves. So much of bad parenting happens when the parent makes parenting about them and not their kids.

Do you know what I mean?

When my identity and name was settled with the Father, it started healing the wound of my father inside of me. That moment set me free from trying to be the god of my kids' lives, and instead I have become a father who prepares them to be adopted for themselves.

That is your job, Mom and Dad! Whether you are a single parent or not. God the Father wants to be your kids' father as well! When we get out of the way by not projecting our own brokenness upon our kids, it sets them free to be fathered by God themselves. I met a young man the other day who told me he would give anything to hear from his father that he had done something right. "All I hear from my dad is that I am a disappointment to him." Would it surprise you to know that this father was treated the same way by his dad?

Tough or Tight Love?

We hear a lot of talk about "tough love"—about how kids need to learn from their mistakes. One dad said to me recently, "Well, I was a bonehead and did stupid stuff, and my son is just like me."

I asked how close his father was to him when he was struggling as a teenager. "My dad wasn't there at all," he said.

Then I asked, "Do you think it would have gone better for you if your dad had sought you out when you were hurting?"

With tears in his eyes he said, "I would have given anything to have my dad there!"

Isn't that what all of us long for? Isn't that what our children want? And isn't that the way of our heavenly Father, already running toward us in love and delight?

As you've seen in our journey together, we don't need to remain trapped in the brokenness of our fathers and the false names we give ourselves. We can leave behind our family's brokenness *if* we allow our heavenly Father to model for us what true fatherhood looks like. Our new Father will show us how to build a bridge and reach that angry son or daughter who has cut us out of their life . . . yet who at the same time wants more than anything else to have their dad back in their story. Kids need a present, loving father to cross the stormy seas of life. Present fathers are like a lighthouse to a lost ship on a stormy night. Even the best captain can get lost without a lighthouse on the horizon, showing them the way home.

My role as a dad isn't about steering the wheel of my children's lives, but about giving my kids hope that they will make it.

That reminds me of the first steps my son Edward took. I held out my arms to him, and with each attempt he walked farther and farther. I could see a change in his eyes as they met mine. He trusted me enough to go for it . . . and soon he walked across the room. I can't tell you how many times I have felt my Father in heaven do the same thing with me, encouraging me to go beyond my limitations. Although at times my heart has been filled with uncertainty, it has been the look of delight and love on God's face that has compelled me to do things I would have never accomplished without Him.

And when I do—when I finally "walk across the room"—I know I am delighting Him, which makes me want to do even more.

The writer of Hebrews lets us in on the way Jesus lived His life, and finished His race, when he writes, "who for the joy that was set before him endured the cross, despising the shame, and is seated at the right hand of the throne of God" (Heb. 12:2).

Was it the smile on His Father's face that gave Him the courage to take those steps down the Via Dolorosa and carry the cross to His earthly end?

Let me ask you a question. Do you think your kids need the smile on your face right now to help them navigate the storms of life?

Over the years, I've counseled hundreds of young people. They might be in the worst place of their lives. In fact, they might have cut their parents out of their lives! But I have never met a single young person who doesn't, deep down, want their parents back in their lives. They simply don't know how to cross that valley of pain to get back to you. In the same way, we were completely unable to cross the valley to get home to our heavenly Father. God had a plan: He sent His Son to us to bring us home. What's your plan to bring your children home?

If we want to see our families healed and restored, we need fathers and mothers who are willing to pay any price to rescue their lost kids. Lost fathers and mothers can't rescue lost kids. But parents who are named by their heavenly Father and empowered by His Spirit? Well, they can do anything. And I'm here to tell you that as long as your kids are still alive, it is *never* too late. God put this book in your hands to give you hope. You *can* see the family God has given you become everything He intends it to be.

So what's the next step to becoming that kind of father or mother?

The Smile That Says I'm Here

What does the look on your dad's face tell you when you walk into the room?

First of all, if your dad isn't smiling, you know instinctively he isn't approachable. But if he's smiling, it means you are free to interact with him. The smile on our faces is the welcome home sign our kids need to feel safe to approach us. A smile also communicates, "No matter what you're going through, I will be with you every step of the way."

Jesus was empowered to face the mission of His life through the joy that was set before Him. The Father's smile over His life gave Him the courage to "endure the cross" and "despise the shame." Can you imagine being the Creator of the universe and letting the creation that you love reject you and crucify you on the cross? Jesus was able to tap into a level of trust, because He was secure in His Father's pleasure as His beloved Son.

If His relationship with His Father was based on performance, then the cross would have marked the end of a failed ministry. Jesus's disciples scattered and lost hope. His chief financial officer committed suicide and His last moments on earth were shared with two thieves being crucified next to Him. Not a good résumé.

Jesus was connected to something that enabled Him to complete the purpose of His life. I think the love and pleasure of His Father secured His sonship, and no amount of suffering could separate Him from it.

I love the verse in Romans that says, "Who shall separate us from the love of Christ? Shall tribulation, or distress, or persecution, or famine, or nakedness, or danger, or sword?" (Rom. 8:35).

Jesus walked that out, and wants us to live the same way.

Jesus was able to model the love of God to His followers because He first received it for Himself. As a matter of fact, Jesus's relationship with His Father did not begin with His birth on earth. It is eternal. When Jesus became a man, He stepped into uncharted waters. He knew He would not be able to finish His race without a moment-by-moment relationship with His Father. He had no training to fall back on. He didn't go to school and take Being Human 101.

The Creator of the universe allowed himself to be limited by everything it means to be human. Hunger, bodily weakness, rejection by other people . . . all those things were new experiences. So how did He navigate those waters? How did He know which way to choose, which way to go? He turned to His lighthouse, the only One who had the answers. His Father. The rhythm of His life was set every morning by the revelation of His Father's smile for that day.

That is the same way you and I need to live. We need to know that same smile over us, and learn how to follow and trust the Father the same way Jesus did. It is the rhythm of the way a loving dad and his son relate. We live in a culture that practically eliminates the need for a dad, as though the only thing a father does is feed you and give you a safe place to live when you're small. After that, you're on your own. Yet Jesus was over thirty and lived His whole life for His Father's glory and in the glow of His Father's delight.

In my ministry, I meet people every day who miss their dads, who wish they could have just one more day together. Sometimes the folks who miss their dads so badly are dads themselves, or even grandparents. There is never a time we don't need a father.

Fathered by God

I never had one moment with my dad. That's been hard. But now I have a new Father who is not only in my life now, but will be forever and ever! The formula has to be simple enough for an old football player to grasp, so here it is: the way I am fathered by God is the way I father my kids. And by God's grace, the way I father my kids will continue from generation to generation. The same is true for girls too. The way you are fathered by God will determine the woman you will become and the difference you will make in your loved ones' lives.

That might seem simple to you, but it revolutionized my life as a dad. Fathering my kids the way my heavenly Father loved Jesus and loves me completely changed my relationship with my kids. God has given me a heart for my kids because my search for my identity was satisfied when He renamed me Beloved in front of those high school kids. I was no longer un-fathered. I was given access to as much of the revelation of the Father's love as I was willing to receive, and receiving it every day equips me to be the dad that my kids need in their story. The sweet spot in parenting comes when you have your kids' hearts and they want you to be a part of their story—when they invite you in, share their struggles, and want you to be a part of everything in their lives. Somehow parenting has been reduced to feeding, protecting, and sending out your offspring to make it on their own. I find that kids want their parents in their lives, especially when Mom and Dad are there to speak life and support them with their love.

God's blessing will pass on to your kids to the same degree that you've received it for yourself. The more blessing you *receive* from your Father in heaven, the more blessing you *have* to give to your kids. Guys and gals find it nearly impossible, and always unsustainable, to give what their dads have never given them. Generations of families have passed on the sins of their fathers, rather than passing on the blessings we were designed to give. When Jesus stood in the Jordan River and heard the Father's voice naming Him "Beloved," the blessing of the Father descended upon Him, and that same blessing becomes ours when we are born again. We have the same name that empowered Jesus, because we have been adopted into His Father's family forever. Our main mission as a dad and mom is to extend that same blessing to our children.

When you do that, Beloved, the curse of your absent father is broken.

A Present Father

God the Father is always present with us—and not simply *waiting* for us, either. God is more active. Remember that in the Parable of the Running Father, the father leaps off his porch and runs toward his son *while his son is still a long way off*. Think about that—it means the father was constantly scanning the horizon for his son. He was ready to run toward his son before his son was even aware he could see him.

That's how God acts toward us. He is constantly drawing us home with His love, running toward us to bless us. Wherever we are, whatever we are doing, He is always there. As Psalm 139 says,

> Is there anyplace I can go to avoid your Spirit?
>   to be out of your sight?
> If I climb to the sky, you're there!
>   If I go underground, you're there!
> If I flew on morning's wings
>   to the far western horizon,
> You'd find me in a minute—
>   you're already there waiting! (vv. 7–10 Message)

God, in His great love, has anticipated the journey of my brokenness and is waiting for my slightest turn home to jump off of the porch and run toward me.

You may have been told, like I was, that since God sees everything you do, you need to do the right thing at all times. It's true that we are called to do the right thing, even when no one is watching, but it's not because God is a cosmic Santa Claus who knows when we've been bad or good. God isn't watching us in order to trap us or give us a gold star for good behavior. Instead, God watches us because He delights in His creation. He runs after us because He can't wait to spend time with us. He doesn't try to buy our affection, but instead offers Himself to us. The presence of God is everything we have always wanted. The revelation of the Father and Son and Spirit is so rich, so exciting, so empowering, that it fills us for eternity. The smallest glimpse of that revelation on earth turns the hardest heart into a present, loving person capable of giving his life away in worship and love.

I saw an invitation to a birthday party that noted, *Your presence is our present.* Think about that. The birthday party would be memorable and fun, but not because the guests brought certain presents or spent a certain amount of money. No, it would be a delight because the guests brought *themselves*.

That's how our heavenly Father operates. He blesses us with His *presence*. What we need is a Father who can open wide our horizons, who can bless us by calling us toward the good works He has already prepared for us to do. No matter where we go or what we do, we know that our Father is always with us—and even if we choose to live in "the far country," our heavenly Father runs toward us.

Dads, your families crave your presence. There is a world of difference between providing your family with presence and giving them presents. When we work longer hours so that we can "provide what our family needs," often we are substituting presents for presence. We tell ourselves it's okay when we can't go to our kid's basketball game or piano recital—after all, we paid for new high-tops and the best piano lessons available. But what our kids really want isn't new stuff. It's *us*. They want to look into the stands and see our faces. They want to see us stand up and cheer for them. They want to hear us go crazy with love for them, dancing and singing because we're overflowing with joy. In short, they want to know we are *present*—and if we are present, the latest and greatest *presents* simply won't matter.

Presence versus Presents

My kids, just like yours, are the targets of the world's marketing. Our culture wants to name our kids by what they have or don't have. My challenge as a dad is to be closer to the heart of my kids than the marketers are. If I'm regularly giving myself to them, their identity will come more from relationship than possessions.

But what do you do if you've given more presents than presence? One of the questions that consistently comes up at my conferences is: How do I get my kids back if I've lost them to . . . ?

Maybe what your kids need is to see you jumping off the porch to welcome them home. You will have to get out of your comfort zone to do that. It's undignified to run toward a son who has spent his inheritance and ruined your reputation. The world's way is to make kids pay for their mistakes. God's way knows we are doomed to prodigal living unless He jumps off of the porch of heaven and becomes human and shows us the way back to the Father's house.

This isn't about maintaining your respectability. This isn't about "tough love," which too often becomes an excuse to walk away from our kids and leave them in brokenness, transferring our responsibility to their shoulders. Heaven's version of tough love *pursues* us. I call it "present love," the love that pursues us to bring us back home. Isn't that the way God captured your heart? God's love says, "Ed, no matter how far you run away, I am going to do everything I can to love you back home. My presence will pursue you no matter what you do or where you go."

What would happen if we pursued our broken kids that way, instead of isolating them and demanding they become perfect first?

When I was young, my parents would send me to my room for a time-out when I was bad. One particular day, I had learned a new cuss word. My mom washed out my mouth with soap and told me to go to my room and say every bad word I could to get it out of my system. All I learned in my room were more creative combinations of cuss words, but with bubbles added! I didn't need a time-out so much as I needed someone to recognize the root of the problem. I was acting out (in this instance, using cuss words) because there was something hurting deep inside. (By the way, I learned those words from my sailor stepfather.)

Pursuing our kids is a crucial step in providing them with the fatherly blessing they crave—even if they don't know it or won't admit it. Our presence can make all the difference in the world for our kids, especially when they are broken.

I came home the other day and my son said, "Something just happened and I need to talk to you about it." My heart just skipped a beat, not sure of what he was going to tell me.

He looked at me and said, "Dad, I just got a speeding ticket for going over one hundred miles an hour in the carpool lane, and the police want to talk to you. They might want to impound your car. I am so sorry, but I didn't want to hide anything from you."

My heart was so touched by the fact that he busted himself. That he trusted me enough to not explode over the fact that he made a mistake. In my early years of fathering, it was easy to overreact and treat them like a football player rather than the sons and daughters I love. One of the ways you will know you have the hearts of your children is when they come to you and bust themselves, before you read about it in the paper.

I have had some of the most amazing times with my kids in their brokenness, and it has only been possible because of the way God treats me when I am broken. God didn't rip my face off and say, "Ed, I can't believe that you are still broken, even after My Son died for you!" He is always gentle and loving with me, and that transformation has made me into a different sort of father.

How you speak to your kids and bless them will live beyond you, for generation after generation.

The House That Smiles

Once, after a long day of work, I opened the front door and two things confronted me: the racket of yelling voices and the acidic smell of an unidentified burning object.

My wife ran to meet me. "Come see what *your* son Luke has done!" she said, obviously so distressed by his actions that she momentarily disowned him. I walked into our carpeted garage and immediately realized that the commotion and the awful smell had a common source. Nine-year-old Luke had discovered a new talent with my heat gun: through experimentation, he learned that a heat gun held about an inch above the carpet would melt the carpet fibers together. To ensure that his eureka moment would be remembered throughout posterity, he had spelled out "Lukas" on the carpet. Oblivious to the frantic screams of his mother, he was still finishing up his masterpiece when I arrived.

When he saw me walk in the garage, he looked up at me with a huge grin spread across his face. "What do you think, Dad?" he asked, anxiously awaiting my response.

My first thought was to lay into him—how could he do such a thing? Blessedly, I waited a moment before saying anything, and while I was thinking I looked down and realized just how proud Luke was of his artistic discovery. Finally, much to my wife's dismay, I replied, "Son, you didn't finish the 's.'"

Haven't we all been there, desperate for our father's attention and approval? What is it that compels us to sometimes scrawl our name in the metaphorical carpet with a heat gun? I believe God made us that way, with a longing to be noticed and adored. He gave us a yearning to be loved, seen, and appreciated. Like Luke, we want someone to notice our talents and rejoice over them—and that kind of blessing *always* requires real presence.

We're made for God's smile, our families are made for our smiles, and smiles are always personal.

Have you found yourself disliking your kids when they don't measure up? Or using gifts as a substitute for your fatherly presence? Instead of enjoying my early years of fathering, I kept my kids at arm's length when they weren't performing to their potential. The more I scolded them, the more fear shaped the way they were living. The Bible teaches us that perfect love produces courage, not fear. When I saw that my kids were living in fear of disappointing me, I knew my love was about a million miles from perfect. Ouch!

What is the atmosphere in your home like? If your kids don't think that you like them, it will be almost impossible for them to feel your love. The Bible teaches us in Psalm 16:11 that "in [God's] presence is fullness of joy; at Your right hand are pleasures for-evermore" (NKJV). In other words, you can either raise your kids from the right hand of your pleasure, or you can pass on the frown that most of us got from our fathers. God the Father smiles over you, always.

His smile isn't because you're perfect, and it doesn't change depending on how well you perform. Is that how you treat your family? Are you a present father, or do you substitute presents for yourself? When you are present with your family, do you enjoy them? Does your love for and delight in your family call out their courageous best?

The next time your kids wonder what you think about them, make sure they picture your smile.

Are you ready for the Father you've always wanted?

Father time . . .

Father, I thank You that from the beginning of my story You have waited for the day of my adoption in Your family. I accept that You chose me to be Your Beloved one and that I am no longer stuck in my father's house because I now have You—the Father I have always wanted—and I receive You as my Father. I will commit myself to spending time with You every day so I can learn about the inheritance that Jesus purchased for me. Being Your son or daughter is now my new sweet spot. Keep my heart fixed on You as Your love and smile is now my compass for my way home to the Father's house! ☺

11

Building a House with
God's Smile

It is your Father's good pleasure to give you the
kingdom.

Luke 12:32

A New Vision

When I sat down to write this book, I wanted to do two things:
position you to encounter the Father you've always wanted so that
the wound of your father could be healed, and give you hope that
your family can become everything God wants it to be.

I can't tell you how often I've heard someone say, "I really blew
it as a dad! I wish I could start over with my kids!" The secret is
that you can! No matter what age you are, or what ages your kids
are, they are still waiting for your smile over their life. They are

still waiting to live in a father's house that is full of love and de-light—the same kind of house our heavenly Father has prepared for His beloved children.

So how do you build a house that has God's smile over it? How do you as a single mom build the same kind of house without an earthbound dad?

You've already taken the first step. Once you discover you were chosen by the Father in heaven to be adopted and renamed Beloved, it begins to set you free from your quest for the blessing you have needed so that you can now give that same blessing toward your kids.

One of the first things the Father revealed to me was how stingy I had been with my affection toward my own kids. I was uncomfortable loving them because my heart had been taught that love was payment for performance. It took the generosity of the Father's unconditional, everlasting, preexisting love to melt away my need to prove myself to God and to change the audience of my life to an audience of One.

Even though I knew God's love was unconditional, I struggled to love others without a price tag. Performance for love was down-loaded to me in almost every relationship as a child. The whole world runs on performance-based love. And plenty of kids today don't even have a father to try performing for! Almost half the kids born in America don't have a father around. Over 41 percent of all children born in our country in 2011 were born to unwed mothers. Nearly three quarters of African American children, half of Latino babies, and 29 percent of Caucasian babies are born outside mar-riage. A disturbing trend, compared with the craziness of the '60s when less than 25 percent of babies were born to unwed mothers. When this generation of kids looks to the stands, at least half of them will see another empty seat.

A New Heart

So what is heaven's response to this tragedy? Jesus prayed a road map for every orphan heart, giving them the home and family they need. "Father, I desire that they also, whom you have given me, may be with me where I am, to see my glory that you have given me because you loved me before the foundation of the world" (John 17:24). His prayer was an invitation into a new way of living. It was an invitation into the same relationship of being absolutely loved that Jesus had with His own Father.

Jesus goes on to pray that we will see God's glory. I believe this verse reveals that God's glory is His visible love. The word "see" is also translated "experience." In other words, the way we can rebuild our lives is to see and experience the love of the Father.

You can change the way someone looks by loving them. I have watched that happen in my wife's face. When she feels loved by me, she glows and releases her beauty. But if she isn't feeling it . . . well, let's say a subtropical depression starts to form. You can look at the face of a young person and tell if they are loved. There is a certain way they carry themselves, a confidence to risk, and a willingness to live life that is a manifestation of being loved. I wish I could tell you that I see a lot of kids who carry themselves that way. I don't. Instead I see a generation of orphans who have never experienced being loved and adored by a father.

Do you feel more connected to God when you are present with your family? Do you feel more connected to your family when you love them for their sake? Or is your heart more satisfied when others make a big deal out of you?

It was the Father's unrelenting pursuit of *me* that showed me life was really about loving *others*.

One of the most extraordinary things about being named Beloved by the Father is that for the first time I felt chosen, loved, and no longer invisible. I had this feeling of relief. Like I had been searching all of my life for my Father that I lost, and saw Him instead running towards me to restore everything that I lost. He chose to love me by calling me His Beloved and I didn't have to have it together to be included in His family.

That generous moment with the Father I have always wanted opened my heart to the gift of loving others the way God loves me. There is nothing sweeter in life than loving someone for their sake and not your own. It takes no courage to be selfish and make love all about you. It takes great courage, however, to love someone truly, because true love requires risk, and risk makes you vulnerable. God loved the world so much that He gave His only Son. God modeled sacrificial love, and He designed us to love others the same way.

A New Home

How does the Father bring an orphan heart home that has been wandering for years? Jesus talked about this home as the Father's house. "There is plenty of room for you in my Father's home. If that weren't so, would I have told you that I'm on my way to get a room ready for you?" (John 14:2 Message). It's one thing to *tell* someone you love them—but it's another thing entirely to invite them to move in with you and it is another thing altogether to invite them to move into a house you have designed for thousands of years to love them with! Your adoption also comes with a home, which has been crafted and designed just for you.

When Jesus promised, "I will not leave you as orphans," He was talking about His mission. He came to seek and save the lost, finding and returning everyone who was stolen by the devil out of His Father's house. Everything God has done in history has been done for the sake of His family. Family is at the core of all

God's truth, and even the Trinity is a picture of family in loving relationship.

The core of most people's pain on earth is a broken family. God's healing answer is His new family. The devil thinks that his strategy of destroying fathers will stop the kingdom of God from advancing. But he hasn't read Malachi 4:6, which records God's promise to "turn the hearts of fathers to their children." I am watching this promise come true. The blessing of the Father in heaven is equipping boys to become men, girls to become women, men to become fathers, women to become mothers, and parents to bless their children.

I believe that's the direction God is pointing your heart as well. Hasn't the love of the Father been wooing and drawing you into His love over your life? Have you spent much of your life looking for the healing from the wounds of your father? I did. How about you?

Building your house around the smile of God starts with you, *because you cannot give what you have never received.* Your children will reap what you sow into them, and the seeds of love and blessing will be given to you when you are named and transformed by your heavenly Father. Jesus said, "A good tree cannot bear bad fruit, nor can a bad tree bear good fruit" (Matt. 7:18 NKJV). When Jesus challenged Nicodemus that, for him to be able to enter this new life, he had to be "born again," he didn't need another sermon or another principle to lead his life with. He needed to fundamentally become an entirely different person. In other words, he needed to have a completely new family root system to draw his life from. The old family tree was not capable of producing the good fruit that Jesus was promising him.

Jesus said, "I am the vine; you are the branches. Whoever abides in me and I in him, he it is that bears much fruit, for apart from me you can do nothing" (John 15:5). In other words, the moment you were born again, the root system of your old family was cut off and the tree of your life was grafted into your new family with the promise of a new life filled with the blessing of fruitfulness.

One of my favorite movies gives us a picture of this. *A Walk in the Clouds* is the story of a young soldier raised in an orphanage who finally meets a family that he has always wanted. At the end of the movie, a fire burns down the family vineyard. Thinking all is lost, the young soldier discovers that the fire only burned the branches and not the root system of the original vine the family brought from the old country. The father then cuts off a root clipping and says, "This . . . is the root . . . of your life . . . the root . . . of your family. You are bound to this land . . . and to this family . . . by commitment . . . by honor . . . and by love." The young soldier was an orphan no more because the root of his old life had been burned away and the new root was his destiny.

That's exactly what Jesus is to us. He is the root of our new family. "There shall be a root of Jesse; And He who shall rise to reign over the Gentiles, in Him the Gentiles shall hope" (Rom. 15:12 NKJV). Jesus came to graft us into the root of the Father's new family. No longer are you Orphan, but Beloved. That is the legacy of love you can—you must—leave to your family.

Letting Go of the Old

Did you know that you can encounter the same Father who loved and blessed Jesus? Everything we see in the life of Jesus flowed from His relationship with His Dad. His trust, faith, love, and power came through that relationship. He not only came to model that life, He also came to make it possible for us to live that same way. I have met many in my journey who are still looking for a father to help them fix the broken reality inside their hearts. There are a lot of people out there trying to speak into this universal father wound that crosses every culture. Only Jesus offers us the Father we have always wanted, who at the moment of us being born again, changes our root system to being rooted in love with the promise of a life filled with His joy, love, and peace.

That's not the same as an easy life, as any parent knows. But it is the best life.

So how do we receive it for ourselves? We need to exchange our old family root system for a new one. Nothing short of an extreme makeover will turn your house into one with God's smile over it. You must move out and turn over the keys of your life to God's extreme makeover team. The popular show *Extreme Makeover* represents the best of human ability to build a house from scratch, and if that's the best we can do, just imagine what the Father's house will look like after thousands of years of construction! I believe that the construction crews are in their final preparations, and God can't wait for the day when Jesus stands up from His throne and finally shouts over the heavens, "Move that bus!"

Do you feel the pursuit of the Running Father right now? The first step to rebuilding your home is not to slap on another coat of paint . . . it's to start over from the ground up. What does your house look like right now? Have you built your family around you? One of the quickest ways to measure the way you are loving your family is to look at your relationship with them. The degree of love that shines off of your family will reveal the condition of the way you have been building your house. I wrote earlier about the day God gave me a snapshot of my life. It was one of those horrible/wonderful days—horrible in that I saw how focused on myself I was, and wonderful in that I still had time to turn things around.

Your kids wake up every day wondering what you think of them. If your life is a house, what does it look like?

To rebuild your life, you must first allow God to bulldoze it. You need to be rebuilt the Father's way. If you're ready, the next step is to confess that you can't rebuild your own life without Him. You're patching the walls on a house that needs to be torn down. The day my life was torn down was the day a young campus pastor invited me to pray a prayer with him that I'm going to invite you to pray as well. That wasn't the day I became perfect—that day will never come on this earth, as my wife and kids can testify! That was the day, however, when God's love became real to me, and that's the foundation of any house over which the Father's smile shines like the sun.

Can I ask you a question right now? Where is your relationship with Jesus and His Father? Have you ever totally given your life back to Him to rebuild? You can do that right now. How?

Ask Him with me through this prayer:

Father, I confess to You right now that I cannot heal my life or my family. I have sinned against You, and have hurt those whom I love. I was born spiritually dead and I want to be born again so I can know what it is like to be completely loved by You. I want to know what it is like to be Your beloved son or daughter. I give You my broken heart. Give me a new heart so I can love others the way You love me. Jesus, open my heart right now to the Father I have always wanted so that I can build the rest of my life on Your love and blessings. In the name of Jesus, amen!

If you just prayed that prayer and meant it, would you send me an email right now (fathers@mac.com) and tell me about your decision—I would love to hear from you!

Becoming a Son or Daughter

Congratulations, Beloved! I prayed a prayer just like that one in 1977 and a whole new world started opening for me. His love for me was so much greater than anything I have ever imagined. The Scripture says, "No eye has seen, nor ear heard, nor the heart of man imagined, what God has prepared for those who love him" (1 Cor. 2:9).

You have just invited the Creator of the universe into your story. He loves to turn broken stories into miracles. He specializes in turning invisible people into the shining lights of this world. "He decided from the outset to shape the lives of those who love him along the same lines as the life of his Son" (Rom. 8:29 Message).

Your life is now about what is ahead of you and the adventure the Father has designed for you.

The next step to building the smile of God over your life and family is to receive the blessing that the heavenly Father has for you. When Jesus went down in the Jordan River, baptism was symbolic of a new life. The Bible calls it being born again. You have just been born again into the Father's family and become the son or daughter God destined you to be. You might have spent your life alone, separated with no family. But that is not true anymore. God has wanted to be the Father of your new story.

I love what Romans 8:15 says: "For you did not receive the spirit of slavery to fall back into fear, but you have received the Spirit of adoption as sons, by whom we cry, 'Abba! Father!'"

In Christ you are a beloved son or daughter and no longer an orphan. Jesus, the Great Physician, has the only cure for an un-fathered heart. His cure is none other than the Biggest Papa of all time, "Abba Father!" When Paul used the word "adoption," it was filled with some incredible truths. In Rome, a parent could get rid of their birth children if they wanted to, but at the moment of legal adoption, that child could never be rejected. That child became *more* than their natural child because they were chosen to be adopted. Paul is saying, in essence, "God chose you and His choice is permanent!"

Also, at the moment you were born again a miracle happens inside of you. The Bible says that you become a new kind of person through the supernatural work of the Spirit of God in you. The Spirit of adoption is deposited in your heart as your new adoptive Father now becomes your new birth Father and you now become His son or daughter. "You can tell for sure that you are now fully adopted as his own children because God sent the Spirit of his Son into our lives crying out, 'Papa! Father!'" (Gal. 4:6 Message). In other words, your family history has just changed, because now your heart cries out in joy that you are no longer an orphan but you have the Father you have always wanted!

That's the miracle that Jesus's sacrifice bought for us on the cross. The Bible says, "For as by one man's disobedience many were made sinners, so also by one Man's obedience many will be made righteous" (Rom. 5:19 NKJV). What Adam did in the garden was completely reversed by the obedience of Jesus on the cross, and the Father who lost us to sin can now adopt us and give us the life He always wanted us to have. The revelation that your heavenly Father has become your birth Father changes everything in your life.

Becoming a New Father or Mother

Now that your identity is intact, how do you transfer that to the way you father or mother your kids?

Do you remember the first words your kids spoke? I was in my study when Jill said, "Ed, come quick, Edward just said his first word." I ran into the room as Jill was trying to get him to say it again. After about twenty attempts, my firstborn said it.

"Dada."

Few things are more precious to a father than to have his kids want him in their life. And Dada, like "Abba," is one of those words that not only speaks about the relationship between a father and son; it also sets the terms for intimacy. Jesus used the name Abba to describe the kind of relationship we can have with God the Father. The intimacy a son and daughter can have with their father is one of the most powerful relationships imaginable, and that's exactly what we're being invited into: God to us, and us to our children.

There is also nothing more painful for a father and his kids than a relationship on the rocks. My deepest struggles as a dad have come when I've made my parenting about me. That's the quickest way to drive your kids away from you. My struggle wasn't because I didn't love them. I did. My struggle was about my own identity and feeling as though I didn't have what it took to be a good dad.

I was the son of a Navy pilot who died in action, the stepson of a commander of a submarine, and the grandson of a three-star admiral. I was expected to achieve and name myself to prove their sacrifices hadn't been in vain. My days in the NFL, my world-record bench press, my fishing career, the many hobbies I distracted myself with—all that came from a place in me that was trying to prove myself. All of the men in my family named themselves by their achievements, so I thought I had to as well.

When you try to prove yourself worthy of love and respect, you place that same pressure on your kids. You're setting up your kids for the same struggles that have plagued you. The name you carry will be the name you transfer to your children.

You have a new name now. Bless your kids and set them free to be a beloved son or daughter—first beloved by you, and ultimately beloved by their heavenly Father.

Beloved

Are you ready to let go of the things you have named yourself and receive the new name the Father wants to give you?

You will no longer be called _____ [*insert the names you label yourself with*].

Now you are Beloved.

The loss of my father in the waters off Monterey and the questions that haunted my heart were answered when the blessing of my new Father called me to be the man I was destined to be. I wondered most of my life what it would have felt like to be able to talk to my dad. To hear him say the things he loved about me. To hear him say, "Son, today you are a man, and I want you to know you have what it takes." That didn't happen for me until I was forty years old. It wasn't my dad, Ed Tandy, who called me out. It was the same voice that spoke over Jesus at the Jordan River.

From before your birth, God has shaped your life so He can reveal His love to you. He has been waiting for the moment you catch His loving gaze and hear His voice. He knows it is impossible for us to change unless we are saved by His Son, named by Him, and empowered by His Spirit. The truth of our journey isn't how we start the race, but how we finish. When the rock that covered Jesus's tomb rolled away, it opened the door to the orphanage that Adam and Eve built for us. The father of lies lost his power to name us, and we were adopted into a new family that we'll live with forever in God's house.

The Father longs for a day when there are no more orphans and His house is filled with His restored family. That's the dream I have given my life to as well, and every time a father returns to his family, another orphan is restored.

The miracle your family needs is eighteen inches below your head: get a new heart. When you give your heart to God, He loves it so well that your heart can love others the same way He has loved you. To be wanted, to belong, and to be blessed by a father is one of the deepest longings we're born with. You might have thought that could never happen to you because your dad is either gone or too broken to bless you. You might have thought you could never bless your children like that because you don't know how.

Beloved, it's never too late. My graduation into manhood didn't come by climbing a mountain, winning a big game, or kissing my first girl. It came the moment the Father's voice named me and His Spirit empowered me to become the man, husband, and father I had always wanted to be. It was—and is—a long journey. It isn't always easy. But there's no place I'd rather be than living beneath the smile of my heavenly Father, and passing that smile on to my children and family.

I Want to Be Your Father

Do you hear your name being called? God is ready for another son or daughter to come home to the Father's house.

The Son has come to save you, the Father is ready to name you, and the Holy Spirit is poised to empower you with the same wisdom, stature, and favor that Jesus enjoyed.

Remember the dog tags my father Ed Tandy took off and laid on my mother's bedside table? I have wondered for years if the Scripture that he read the night before gave him a premonition of the last moments of his life. My mother left the dog tags to me in her will and I have worn them ever since. I was preaching in an event at a conference center in the South this year. When I stood to walk up on the stage, my dog tags jingled. They must have jingled a million times around my neck, but this time God spoke to my heart in that moment and said, "I allowed your father to come home early so I could be your Father—so that those who hear this message won't be able to say that you received this from your earthly father."

Those words rocked me to my core as He answered my biggest question about why my dad died before I was born. I felt like Joseph did in the Bible when he was able to see God's plan through the pain. He said to his brothers, "Don't you see, you planned evil against me but God used those same plans for my good, as you see all around you right now—life for many people" (Gen. 50:20 Message).

God is the only one who can take what's been stolen from us and turn it into a testimony for His glory. He found an orphan boy named Ed at forty years old and fathered me in a way that gives hope to those who lost their fathers.

What is the story of your life that needs the Father's blessing to heal?

God loves to turn our broken stories into a testimony of His love and power. Like so many others without a dad's blessing, God worked out my story for the good, and He is the only Father who can change your story too. He also said to my heart in that moment, "Go and tell them that I love them and sent my Son to let them know that I am the Father they have always wanted."

I wrote this book to introduce you to the only Father who can change your story. As one of His beloved sons, I am here to testify that I have missed nothing losing my father in that plane crash, because I got the Father that I have always wanted, and He wants to be your Father too.

Now it is time for your new name—this is your adoption day at the Father's house. He has planned for all of eternity to adopt you back from the father of lies and move you into the eternal family that He is building. The beloved! You will be an orphan no more. Are you ready? Your heavenly Father's perfect love is the only thing that conquers our fear, forgives our sins, restores our hope, and transfers the power of His grace inside of us. He did this at the resurrection of Jesus from the dead. Jesus told His disciples that He would be buried and would rise from the dead but no one understood His words. When Jesus spoke His final words, "It is finished," the price had been paid in full with His death, and the promise and power of us being born again happened at His resurrection.

Mary Magdalene, after hearing that the tomb was empty, came running in hopes of finding the man who pulled her life out of ruin, and she stood there weeping because the tomb was empty. She thought that someone had taken Jesus's body away, when all of a sudden Jesus spoke to her and said,

> "Woman, why do you weep? Who are you looking for?" She, thinking that he was the gardener, said, "Mister, if you took him, tell me where you put him so I can care for him." Jesus said, "Mary." Turning to face him, she said in Hebrew, "*Rabboni!*" meaning "Teacher!" (John 20:15–16 Message)

In three-dimensional, living color, Jesus was standing outside the tomb that represented the father's house we were born into. Jesus then said, "Don't cling to me, for I have not yet ascended to the Father. Go to my brothers and tell them, 'I ascend to my Father and your Father, my God and your God'" (John 20:17 Message).

Beloved, from that moment Jesus gave us a way to never be limited or stuck in the wounds of our fathers. The price for our brokenness was paid on the cross, and the resurrected Son opened a door into the Father's presence that had been closed by Adam and Eve's sin against God. No longer would the children that the Father has wanted to adopt be forever lost in the house of the father of lies. Jesus ascended to the Father who now becomes our Father, and to God who now becomes our God.

It is time to come home to the Father's house, Beloved!

Are you ready for the Father you've always wanted?

Father time . . .

The next step in your story is to get in the river with Jesus and listen for the same voice that blessed Him over two thousand years ago. Open your hands, beloved one, the Father wants to say something to you!

"Hello, My beloved one. I have waited all of eternity for this moment in your story to tell you how much I love you. I perfectly designed you for the dream that I have had in my heart for your life. Long before I laid the earth's foundations, I had you in mind and settled to make you the focus of My love, to make you whole and holy by My love. Before time began, I decided to adopt you into My family through My Son Jesus, so that you will never have to do life alone again.

From this moment on, your name will no longer be about what you have named yourself by, the brokenness of your story, the things you never received from your father, or what you have done against Me. I sent My Son to pay for everything that has separated you from My love. From this moment you are no longer an Orphan, because you are My beloved son, My beloved daughter, whom I love. I have chosen you to be Mine so I can bless you with every spiritual blessing that I have in the heavenly places. You are fatherless no more, because I AM THE FATHER YOU HAVE ALWAYS WANTED!

With My Son in your heart, My name BELOVED upon your life, and My Spirit empowering you, nothing will be impossible for you. Now rise up out of this river of blessing and bless everyone I send your way. I want My house full! Welcome home, Beloved."

Epilogue

The Father's Game Plan to Winning Back Your Family

> Bless—that's your job, to bless. You'll be a blessing
> and also get a blessing.
>
> 1 Peter 3:9 Message

It has been almost twenty years since I did my first conference about the blessing of the Father. We have seen tens of thousands of people just like you receive the blessing that so many of our fathers were so ill-equipped to pass on into our lives. One of the sweetest times at every conference is the question-and-answer time that we have at the end. I have had the feeling at many a conference standing in front of these moms and dads, single men and women, that I might have been the first father figure they have ever approached with the questions that they need answers for.

Here are a few of the most asked questions we have fielded over the years.

1. How do I walk out this blessing every day for the rest of my life?
2. How do I live in my new name now, after I have built my whole life and family on performance?
3. How do I, as a single mom, raise my boys without a father in their lives?
4. How do I repair a broken relationship with my kids after having been absent for most of their lives?
5. How do I bless my kids if they don't want to have anything to do with me?
6. How do I balance work and my time with my kids? Our corporate culture demands so much of my time that I don't have much left when I get home.
7. How do I reach a daughter who hates me? We haven't spoken for years!
8. How do I win back the family I lost in my divorce?
9. How do I reach out to my dad who has caused so much pain in my life?
10. How do I repair my marriage from years of making it about myself?
11. How do I rebuild my family around the blessing of the Father?
12. How do I speak life into my husband while he is still so immature?
13. My husband had a wicked father and it has affected our marriage. How do I reach him when he has told me that he would never come to church and be a part of it?
14. How do I bless my stepchildren as they have been so wounded by their father?
15. How do I minister this blessing to my wife who was repeatedly abused by the men in her life? I feel as though there is part of herself that she keeps hidden from our life together.

These are just a few of the questions that people have had working out their new identity and name that the Father has bestowed upon His children. I call these sessions at the conference "Conversations with My Father."

This came out of my own quiet time that I started having with the Father where I would write out questions to my new Father in prayer and leave a blank space in my journal for His answer. Some of those answers came in the form of Scripture, an insight, a word from another person, an answer to prayer, a great question from a life coach, etc. Much of what I have shared with you has come out of a private, ongoing conversation with Jesus and His Father that has been going on for many years. I would love to invite you into this conversation as well!

If you will go to www.edtandymcglasson.org, you will find the answer to these questions and also meet many more people on the journey with you to the Father's house.

In His smile,
Ed Tandy McGlasson

Notes

Introduction

1. Raniero Cantalamessa, *Life in Christ: A Spiritual Commentary on the Letter to the Romans*, trans. Frances Lonergan Villa (Collegeville, MN: Liturgical Press, 1997), 7.

Chapter 2 The Narrow Horizon of My Father's House

1. *The Five Heartbeats*, directed by Robert Townsend, 20th Century Fox, 1991.
2. David Blankenhorn, *Fatherless America* (New York: Basic Books, 1995), 1.

Chapter 4 What Did Your Father Name You?

1. James Ryle, *Released from the Prison My Father Built* (Franklin, TN: Truthworks, 2010), 21.

Chapter 7 The Trap of Making a Name for Yourself

1. H. G. Wells, *Experiment in Autobiography* (New York: Macmillan, 1934), 52–53. Quoted in Paul Vitz, *Faith of the Fatherless: The Psychology of Atheism* (Dallas: Spence, 1999), 51.

Chapter 8 Meeting My Father

1. C. S. Lewis, *Surprised by Joy: The Shape of My Early Life* (Orlando, FL: Harcourt, 1955), chap. XIV.

Ed Tandy McGlasson is a former lineman in the National Football League where he played with the Giants, the Jets, and the Rams. Ed's call to ministry began in college after being healed from a career-ending knee injury that led to his conversion while playing for Youngstown State. Ed eventually entered the ministry in 1984 and started traveling and sharing his testimony and doing evangelistic crusades. In 1988 Ed planted the Stadium Vineyard in Anaheim, California, and has been a pastor there since.

Ed has spoken at numerous conferences across the country and around the world, including a number of rallies for Billy Graham crusades. Ed's first book, *The Difference a Father Makes*—which has over 200,000 copies in print—along with his conference The Blessing of the Father, keeps Ed busy in churches, conferences, and corporate events.